These are our memories, from our perspective, and we have tried to represent events as faithfully as possible.

ISBN   979-8-9868600-0-8   (paperback)
ISBN   979-8-9868600-1-5   (Kindle)

Library of Congress Control Number: 2022916256
First paperback edition October 2022

Cover design by Olivia Lauren Robinson
Interior design by Anton Khodakovsky

Kindred Souls Publishing
P.O. Box 34-1389
Lakeway, Texas 78734

ANGRY WOMEN

23 ESSAYS ABOUT HIDDEN TRUTHS,

BIG FEELINGS, AND UNEXPECTED WISDOM

Kindred Souls
PUBLISHING

CONTENTS

DEDICATED TO

ALL ANGRY WOMEN EVERYWHERE.

INTRODUCTION

W E BELIEVE IN THE ALCHEMY OF WRITING. *ANGRY WOMEN* is a book, of course, but for many of the twenty-three women who've contributed personal essays about anger, it has been more than a writing project. Over the course of this journey, it became a form of collective healing. Through writing, gathering, sharing, and rewriting, we each wrestled with our anger, eventually forming a new relationship with and understanding of this important emotion. Along the way, we also reached a deeper understanding of all of the other emotions that are often expressed in its place or lurking underneath.

Though the perspectives in this book are both varied and personal, there are some common themes: Women aren't taught to hold anger well. Women are judged for being angry. And yet, many women feel extremely angry—in fact, they're fucking pissed. Centuries of living under the thumb of patriarchy take a toll on the women who must conform to live under these rules, and this toll has an even greater impact on women of color and other intersectional identities based on sexual orientation, gender identity, religion, race/ethnicity, etc. For women with something to say, *Angry Women* became somewhere to say it.

It all started with three friends catching up over Zoom in October 2021. The three of us live in different cities and have regularly gathered online for years. With COVID, of course, Zoom became the norm, and at this difficult time, we welcomed the deep connection.

On this particular day, we were all angry.

At what? Who can remember the specifics? We were angry at the world, at work, at our partners. We were especially angry at failing systems, at living in a patriarchal, racist, and oppressive world. We'd been angry before, but there was something about the confluence of our anger at that moment that made us want to do something about it. Five years before, we'd actually started meeting with the intention of being a writing group, but just checking in and hanging out had subverted any creative agenda. Over the years, we often joked that we were a writing group that never wrote, but that October day, we decided to write about our anger.

We felt like all of the women around us were frustrated, livid, and overwhelmed during the pandemic, but we had no idea what to do with these feelings. We knew that we had trouble expressing anger, often avoiding, diminishing, or otherwise smothering it. We felt that way often, so we wanted to make a change. We wanted a chance to find our voices, and we had a hunch others would, too.

We called this project "Angry Women" and invited our networks to participate: "*Angry Women* will be a self-published book of essays by women around the theme of anger, and we're inviting you to contribute!" We asked these women to commit to writing an essay on the theme of anger. Gatherings were optional, and our goal was the published book you're now holding in your hands. Our call struck a chord: we heard from many women who were eager to join us, as well as many other women who wanted to but were too overwhelmed to devote time to writing at that moment.

We wanted to welcome all perspectives. Anger can look like frustration, righteous anger, rage, indignation, wrath, fear of anger, and so many other things. We intentionally left a big opening for writers to encourage diversity of thought, new perspectives, and multiple ways of approaching this topic. We asked for pieces that revolved around the idea of anger, had clear writing, and contained enough emotional processing that the piece itself wasn't an angry rant. In the end, twenty-three of us came together, and *Angry Women* became a group project, a collective cry, an offering, and a way to have some fun.

For all of us, the process has been one of examining our relationships with anger, seeking understanding, clarity, challenge, collaboration, and expression. Many wanted to look at or find the energy of anger. Some have explored anger through the lens of their family of origin. We also discussed our fear of offending people with our anger and our stories.

The twenty-three of us represent a range of perspectives, stories, ages (spanning eleven to seventy-five), ethnicities, sexual preferences, and other intersecting identities. We're grateful for everything that each writer brought forward, their courage in sharing very personal stories, and their vulnerability as they shared a snapshot of these evolving relationships with anger. We learned a lot from the experience, but we've also learned so much from each contributor. This project is a labor of love and is in alignment with our desire to lift up the diverse voices of women to empower a new, liberated future. In that spirit, the group will donate any proceeds from the sale of this book to a nonprofit organization that supports women.

In addition to our writers, several other wonderful people stepped forward to support the project. Thank you, Rebecca

Stevens, for offering a scholarship to increase access to participation. Thank you, Felicia Rich, for your amazing editing support. Thank you, Vanessa Alfaro, for providing an incredible workshop to help us process and express this powerful emotion.

During the workshop, Vanessa shared that anger is an opportunity to learn about ourselves. We hope that you, too, will learn about yourself through these words.

Cara, Kat, and Steph
Project Initiators and Lead Editors

THE TROUBLE WE'RE IN

ABIGAIL SOMMERFELD

I NEVER LIKED GETTING IN TROUBLE AS A KID. A LURCHING IN my stomach, a darting panic in my heart, knots in my throat, the flush of fire under my cheeks. I tried to find the fastest way out of any trouble I found myself in and avoided getting into it in the first place. Trouble held no thrill for me; my impulsivity and curiosity found other ways out. A sensitive kid with sharp intuition, I was adept at reading the rules of the room, the subtext of the signals; I gave trouble a wide berth.

As the middle sister, I found outlets for my innate need to test, push, provoke, unload, unleash, and express anger in our micro-society of three. Most of the trouble I got in as a kid stemmed from sisterly conflict. My mother asked for the same gift every year on Mother's Day: a day with no fighting. Rarely could we muster the collective stamina and sustained composure to deliver. With the stakes so high, we would implode early in the day, pointing fingers about who started it, the question of starting it always leading to the escalation of the "it" that would cement the end of our short-lived Mother's Day promise to not do "it."

We were good kids with good heads on our shoulders, and our parents trusted us as such. No curfews, no grounding.

The worst trouble we got into was being sent to our rooms to sit and think about our behavior. We made mistakes; we carried the guilt; we ruptured; we repaired. A safety net of expectations, understanding, and love lay beneath the precarious wobbling, stumbles, and falls of growing up.

While letting down my own parents came with its own brand of discomfort, it was the disappointment of grownups outside of our family that unnerved me the most—something about the juxtaposition of the intimate with the unfamiliar, all the authority without the love. Getting in trouble with teachers, coaches, lifeguards, and shopkeepers all brought on variations of terror and shame. Even the phrase "getting in trouble" was uncomfortable; it's the trouble you cause that gets you into the trouble you're in.

My middle school chorus teacher used to say, "You're not sorry. You're just sorry you got caught!" before sending us out of the room to a catchy little tune on the piano ("Gonna Get Along Without You Now" by Skeeter Davis) and the accompaniment of our peers' chipper voices, giddy with relief that it wasn't them this time. Grownups like her gave me the sense that, while I couldn't always win, there was somehow also less to lose. So, while the sting of being caught (or being sorry we got caught) raised our adolescent hackles as our peers happily sang us out into the hallway, that sort of disappointment felt temporary and collectively endured. It flared hot and then burned right out. We took turns taking the heat.

Of all the grownups and of all the trouble, nothing, and I mean *nothing*, is quite like getting in trouble with Someone Else's Mom. Among the different times that I was in trouble with Someone Else's Mom, I can remember two distinctly. The earlier memory is of a sleepover, a minor offense. An elementary school sleepover, the novelty of it kept us up too late. Someone Else's Mom appeared in the doorway wearing a long silk nightgown and a frown as she hushed us into submission and eventual sleep. The late-night exasperation of Someone Else's Mom, coupled with the recognition that my own mom didn't wear silk nightgowns and the realization that I hadn't really seen any other moms at nighttime, made me uneasy. I wanted to go home, away from the nightgown and away from an unfamiliar house, but mostly away from the anger of Someone Else's Mom.

My other memory of getting in trouble with Someone Else's Mom happens to involve yet another silk nightgown. This time was worse. I was older, knew better, and was much farther from home. Worst of all, I was the sole offender. My friend, her daughter, was off the hook. I was the one who made the mistake; who had been selfish; who let the short-term, free-wheeling, fun part of being a teenager eclipse the responsible and dutiful grownup priorities teenagers are also expected to have. I faced Someone Else's Mom alone. No co-conspirator, no ally, no one else to share the blame. Just Someone Else's Mom, a silk nightgown, and a shame snatching me from my body, space, and time as I floundered in the white water of her anger.

What was it about Someone Else's Mom that's so scary? Was it the nightgown, a symbol of intimacy, privacy, and familiarity? I was seeing someone who was not my mom in their nightgown. Was it the someone else's, the not mine, a symbol of distance and otherness, a sporadic cast member in my sphere of influence? My mom doesn't wear nightgowns. Was it the tribal shame that I was reflecting upon my own family and house? "I don't know the rules in your family, but in this family, we care about safety. So, put on your seatbelt."

Or was it what Someone Else's Mom represented? An angry woman. She didn't belong to me. I didn't belong to her. Not my mother. Not my mother's anger. Someone Else's Mother. Someone Else's Mother's anger. It was as foreign and haunting to me back then as my own anger eventually became to myself.

I was more comfortable with anger as a child and as a young woman. I've been an angry child. Swiping indignant punches at my sister, yelling, "I'm not violent!!" enraged because she called me a big word I didn't know. I've been an angry lifeguard; an angry barista; an angry defender on the soccer field; an angry balladeer on the karaoke stage; an angry teacher; and an angry daughter, sister, mother, and wife.

Somewhere along the way, my relationship with anger changed. It was no longer something that came and went as it pleased. It wasn't something I could scream or cry or sweat out of myself. When it came, it stuck. It burrowed. It had strings attached. It was inconvenient. It made threats to lose people, to make them uncomfortable, to let them down. It was something to avoid, to give a wide berth. Roiling beneath a thin veneer of composure, my own anger started to make me as uneasy as Someone Else's Mom in the dark of Someone Else's house. Anger belonged to other people. I wasn't supposed to see it or feel it. It felt like getting in trouble. I wanted to go home. The problem was that anger was part of home, part of me, and not as easy to avoid.

Anger always shows up; it's what we do with it that gets us in trouble. As a family life coach, I'm in the business of getting people out of the business of rescuing themselves and others from hard feelings. I draw out the rallying cry of our inner children. I ask people: What did anger get to look like in your family of origin? What will anger get to look like in the family you are building? We take attendance of who and what comes up. We listen to what they have to tell us, what they need, and what they want. All feelings are welcome here. Feelings are to be felt, not fixed. People are to be seen, not solved.

And if I'm to believe these truths I am selling, I must apply them to myself. From what hard feelings do I try to rescue myself and others? What are the cries of my rallied inner children? What did anger get to look like for me? What will it get to look like now? When did I stop giving anger permission to exist within me? How long has it been absent? Why did I exile it? What do I have to do to bring it back? What does it want from me, for me?

My own anger feels dangerous, like Someone Else's Mom frowning in a silk nightgown.

My anger loses the battle when the choice is between expressing it and risking disconnection. Expressing anger threatens my connection to others; repressing it threatens my connection to myself. The more I subjugate it for the comfort of others, the less comfortable I get. My own anger sits like the cobbler's kids without shoes, ignored, but right beside me as I craft ways to welcome and nourish it in others.

Something changed once I realized I was severing my connection to myself by not allowing my anger to exist. Parenthood, that experience of watching a piece of your heart walk around outside of your body, is the arena in which I reckon with and recover my exiled parts. I do so with the small, daily, meaningful acts of having my son's back; with a commitment to understand and accept who he is so that he can learn to understand and accept himself; by allowing all feelings to exist and be welcome (even if all behaviors are not); and by advocating for him, even when it's inconvenient.

I'm learning to treat myself the way I do my son. I try my best to walk the walk I talk. It's a practice and a process I'll be working on for as long as I live. I try not to ask my anger to be sorry, or sorry it got caught. I try not to ignore or exile my own anger while welcoming it for and from others. I am making my anger a pair of shoes, piece by piece.

I AM KALI

AUDREY KATHERINE

IMAGES OF THE HINDU GODDESS KALI DEPICT HER WITH HER tongue lolling. One of her many hands holds a severed head with blood dripping from it while another holds a bowl to collect the blood and another holds a bloody sword. She wears a necklace of skulls and a belt of human hands. She is standing atop a man, a god named Shiva, appearing to paralyze him to the ground with the weight of her foot. She is bare-breasted and exudes a raw, sexual energy.

I first saw a variation of this image of Kali when I was about eight years old in the movie *Indiana Jones and the Temple of Doom*, which I was drawn to watch repeatedly for a period of time. It was not until I was an adult in my thirties watching that movie again that I realized Kali was the deity of worship in the scenes where Indiana Jones is held captive and almost killed by a Kali cult (an ignorant, Hollywood misrepresentation of Kali worship involving human sacrifice). As someone who has been continuously magnetized to Kali, I suddenly understood why I had been drawn to watch that movie so frequently as a kid—because of her.

Now, in my forties, while diving deep into inner healing work around anger, I can see how, throughout my life, I unconsciously looked to Kali to express anger that was unsafe for me to express in my childhood. Kali protected my inner child from the anger of my mother and the conflict I was born into between the feminine and masculine, my mother and father. The triangulation I experienced between the two is the root of my suffering.

I often felt bombarded by huge, explosive verbal arguments between my parents. Conflict was at the forefront of their relationship, eventually leading to a communication breakdown when I was fourteen years old. From then until they divorced when I was twenty years old, they, for the most part, stopped talking. They wrote notes to communicate mundane things and had their bedrooms on opposite sides of the house. When they did verbally communicate, it was usually a fight. Tension permeated my home like a thick fog.

My mother was uninhibited in her expression of anger; she often erupted unpredictably and was scary, cruel, and uncontained. Her anger also seeped out in other insidious ways, such as the silent treatment. Since my father usually appeared to be the activator of my mother's rage, to be associated with him in any way, especially when she was angry at him, meant to be cast out of connection with her. Plus, when she was angry at him, she was often more loving and attentive to me. In order to be in her good graces and receive the rays of love, affection, and adoration that often broke through the storm clouds and were as intense and impactful as her rage, I distanced myself from my father.

I also tried to avoid being the target of my mother's temper by being really good, but this came at a cost. I was anxious, hypervigilant, constricted, and withdrawn. My savior was my journal that I began writing in at age fourteen, where I allowed myself to vent my rage about my parents and the impact their dysfunction had on me. That same year, Kali came back into my field of consciousness through Anne Rice's vampire Akasha, who plays center stage in *The Queen of the Damned*.[1] I later learned that Kali served as a model for Akasha, as Kali has a very vampiric quality to her.[2] In one of the many stories of Kali's origin, she sprang from the goddess Durga's forehead to help her demolish the male demons that she was battling. Whenever Durga slew a demon, the blood droplets spawned more demons. Kali "licked the blood that had spilled to the ground, preventing the generation of new demons."[3]

Akasha was an ancient Egyptian queen who was made into the first vampire by a spirit that merged with her soul. After creating other vampires, her need for blood diminished, and she eventually became a living statue, kept safe for centuries by vampire guardians who knew she was the source of their existence. She was aware of what was going on in the world, and she saw what she perceived as the evil that men perpetuated, which involved the destruction of the Earth and the subordination of women. She devised a plan to purge the Earth of 99 percent of the men, leaving a few for breeding purposes. She believed the Earth could be restored to a paradise under her reign as Goddess and with the care of women who would teach the few males who survived new ways of being in the world without violence and oppression. Once this was accomplished, the male population would gradually

---

1   Anne Rice, *The Queen of the Damned* (New York: Ballantine Books, 1998).

2   Katherine Ramsland, *The Vampire Companion: The Official Guide to Anne Rice's "The Vampire Chronicles"* (New York: Ballantine Books, 1993).

3   Georg Feuerstein, *Tantra: The Path of Ecstasy* (Boston: Shambhala Publications, Inc., 1998), 40.

be increased.[4] Like Akasha, "Kali manifested herself for the annihilation of demonic male powers in order to restore peace and equilibrium."[5]

The idea of Akasha and Kali wiping out the male species was a comforting fantasy for me, as my father seemed to me, in my younger years, to be the source of my mother's rage. Thus, if he did not exist, then maybe my life would be more peaceful. And truly, when my father went away on business trips, my mother was calmer. When they divorced, her fiery rage seemed to burn out.

When I was twenty years old, I studied abroad in India for four months. I was officially introduced to Kali in her homeland, and I remember feeling attracted to the invincibility, strength, and empowerment she exuded. When I returned to the US from India, I felt like Kali, which was exemplified in my decision to go on a solo hike on one of the tallest mountains near where I lived. Successfully climbing this mountain further affirmed the inner strength and power I felt. But this was short-lived.

A couple of weeks later, a neighbor informed me that there was a man lingering around the house I shared with some other women, specifically around my bedroom window. The next night, when I went into my bedroom, I saw him staring at me through the window. Then he tried to break into our house. We could see his silhouette through the white curtain over the window of the back door, and we heard him jostling the locked doorknob. We called the police. They arrived quickly, but he disappeared, and I never encountered him again. However, this severed my connection to

---

4   Rice, *The Queen of the Damned;* Ramsland, *The Vampire Companion.*

5   Ajit Mookerjee, *Kali: The Feminine Force* (Rochester, VT: Destiny Books, 1998), 8.

Kali's strength and power. I felt victimized. I experienced flashbacks, heart palpitations, panic attacks, and avoidance behavior. For about a year, I was haunted with an intense fear that I was going to die at any moment.

This event also activated the reverse culture shock I was experiencing but denying. I came back from India feeling very different within myself. However, I pretended as if I never went, trying to hold onto the old me so life could feel "normal" and so I could tolerate the same relationship patterns, thus causing an inner conflict that erupted from the stress of being stalked. It was too triggering for me to live in the same home where I had this terrifying experience, and I ended up moving into a studio apartment by myself. Living alone provided the space I needed to integrate the inner changes that had occurred in India into my external life. However, it was frightening to be living alone at times. I put images of Kali around my place and visualized her in meditations to reduce my fear and to feel protected and cared for.

I began to look for Kali in other women and formed deep, intense relationships with a succession of women who exuded fierceness and nurturing energy. I can see now that my scared inner child, still stuck in my childhood home in my psyche, was trying to procure a protector from my rageful mother and from my father, who instigated her rage.

Eventually, I discovered electronic dance music, the underground club scene, and mind-altering substances that transported my consciousness into realms where I embodied and danced with Kali. I was connected to my sexual and feminine energy and empowerment. The intensity of the underground clubs mirrored the intensity of feelings I felt within myself. Dancing served as an outlet to release the rage stored in my body, creating space for expanded states of bliss, peace, and love that were very healing and a welcome reprieve from the fear and anxiety I carried around.

In my early thirties, I found, and was eventually initiated into, a spiritual community devoted to the worship of Kali. This community was led by a priestess who had been initiated into a Shakta Tantra lineage in India. It was a relief to have my draw to Kali validated. I no longer felt delusional or alone in the profundity of my relationship with this spiritual being. There were others who felt a connection to and who were impacted by her. I learned about rituals, mantra, meditation techniques, and many other spiritual technologies to assist with opening up to this feminine force and the divinity within. I was warned about the potential dangers of this path, as Kali cuts through illusions and facades to reveal the Truth, which, as the priestess of this community said, has the potential to evoke insanity or death.

While I learned a lot and felt grateful to belong to a community that worshiped this being who was so meaningful and sacred to me, I did not feel emotionally safe. Looking back, I recognize that I was reenacting trauma from my childhood. There was an atmosphere that had an eerie resemblance to my mother. Misplaced anger and fear were projected among the community members, leaving everyone walking around on eggshells like I had in my childhood home. I often showed up as my wounded, crippled, anxious child self, unaware of how this child part was running the show and was activated by some of the women in the community. I engaged in self-sabotaging behaviors of not following instructions, not memorizing mantras, and not being prepared for rituals, which caused the priestess and other community members to express overt or covert anger toward me. While I recognize the trauma symptoms that were triggered caused challenges with focus and concentration, I can also see now that I was behaving in ways I unconsciously knew would activate their anger because that was what was familiar to me and, sadly, on some level, I felt like I deserved to be treated that way.

Meanwhile, I was in two separate romantic relationships, one with a man and one with a woman, my inner child trying to heal the conflict between the masculine and feminine and, in essence, bring my parents together in my psyche. However, I was engaging in these relationships from this wounded child part and unconsciously acting out repressed anger I had toward my parents, causing both these relationships to destruct. One day, so much suppressed rage was boiling to the surface regarding deep needs not being met from these relationships that I felt like I was going to explode. This rage within me seemed to manifest that day with a fire burning down my apartment and my Kali temple that was filled with altars to and images of her. While I did not actually cause my home to burn down, the fire was deeply symbolic.

The rage that had boiled over was quickly sublimated by my having to pick up the pieces of my life shattered by the fire. I not only had to move, but I also quit my job and left my spiritual community. And these life-changing events caused me to break up with Kali, having been warned what devotion to her could entail. She brought me to my knees with the loss of my home; my journals; my belongings; and these two intimate, romantic relationships. She cut through many illusions of who I thought I was and how I was acting out outdated belief systems, conditioning, and trauma, causing me to step away from roles as a lover, a partner, a professional, and a tantrika. She forced me to be with me, and I delved deeper into my healing. However, I was still left feeling a lifetime of anger in my cells that I didn't know what to do with, and I continued to turn on myself in self-destructive ways.

Almost a year after the fire, I discovered a mystic named Anaiya Sophia, who helped me to connect more with the compassionate, loving, and nurturing sides of Kali. I traveled to Southern France to spend a week with Anaiya and her male partner, who toured me around various sacred sites associated with Mary Magdalene and the Black Madonna. They provided me with an experience of human beings, a feminine and masculine energy, who held me in compassion, love, and safety. Anaiya provided guidance to perform the inner, sacred marriage of the masculine and feminine through various meditation techniques, visualizing these aspects within me coming together in support and harmony.

Anaiya Sophia also taught me about "sacred rage," which she described as "an explosion of wildfire that is both appropriate and timely. It is an in-your-face obliteration of everything that is untrue, unjust, and wrong on every level. It is not a personal form of anger; it is bigger than that. It comes in widescreen and technicolor as it galvanizes its power from the natural world and is often connected to the innocent and undefended. It is thunderous. It is free. And it is so desperately needed. Only the feminine within us can surrender to this innate quality."[6] Anaiya says that "the problem for many of us women growing up is that we are conditioned to not be angry. From a young age, we are encouraged to be nice, pretty, agreeable, quiet, and smiley. Many of us were not taught the

---

6   Anaiya Sophia, *Fierce Feminine Rising: Heal from Predatory Relationships and Recenter Your Personal Power* (Rochester, VT: Destiny Books, 2020), 124.

value of healthy anger, let alone the importance of sacred rage. We were not held or taught by the feminine to be *fully feminine*."[7]

Anaiya calls out to women to allow Kali to enter our bodies and express this sacred rage to help stop the destructive forces of the patriarchy. "Kali is the Dark Mother who is here to awaken her crazed and psychotic children, and She will use anything within Her power to transform us. She is simply saying, 'Either learn what I am trying to teach you, either accept what I am trying to give you, either burn with my passion for justice and transformation—or die out.'"[8]

As I was integrating this wisdom, I met a woman named Vanessa Alfaro. When I saw her dancing, an image of Kali flashed before my eyes. I introduced myself to her, and I learned that she was an anger and communication coach. She had developed a process for releasing anger called the Anger Algorithm.[9] Soon, I began working with her, and I finally started the journey of releasing this lifetime of anger.

Since accessing this channel of anger in me, my awareness has heightened regarding how unhealed wounds from my childhood linked to repressed anger toward my parents keep me stuck in the past, causing me to destructively act out in my current adult relationships whenever these wounds get touched. Recently, I started to intentionally release this repressed anger from my body and psyche using the Anger Algorithm and other therapeutic modalities. As I do this, I find that I am clearer and more present, able to see my relationships as they are as opposed to through a filter from the past.

---

7   Anaiya Sophia, *Fierce Feminine Rising,* 124-125.

8   Anaiya Sophia, *Fierce Feminine Rising,*131.

9   "Vanessa Alfaro," accessed July 2, 2022, https://vanessaalfaro.co/.

This creates greater space for harmony and peace within myself and in my relationships. My heart feels more open and less defended, allowing my capacity for love to grow. With this healing work I am doing, along with distance and boundaries, my relationship with my parents continues to evolve.

Since the fire, I have not restored any images of Kali around me. While I still feel reverence for her and still appreciate her representation of the protective force of anger to set boundaries and meet needs, I no longer need external protection and support. I am learning to create safety for myself, within myself, and I am practicing—though sometimes imperfectly—using the tools I have acquired to express my anger in a healthy, constructive way. Kali is no longer separate from me. I am Kali.

CRASHING INTO ANGER

CARA CARRILLO

'M A "NICE" PERSON, THE ONE WHO SWOOPED IN WITH A SUR-
prise entrance into this upside-down world ten years after
my middle sister was born with a mission to help everybody
in the family get along. As natural as breathing air, I came to
anticipate the feelings and reactions of others, orchestrating
scenarios that would lead to less likelihood of an aggressive
fallout. I knew how most family members were feeling before
they did and observed the tactics my older sisters would uti-
lize to escape or instigate our father's rage. This nurturing
aspect of my personality, punctuated by a Sun sign in Cancer,
led to the nickname "Care (a) Bear." Care Bears were badass,
so far as I was concerned. They all connected their super-
charged hearts to head out into the world to battle evil and
promote love and kindness.

Between my constant need to people please and society's
expectation of me as a woman, I learned early on that there
was no room in this world for an angry Care Bear. Anger was
reserved for rageful fits by men like my father or my sisters'
boyfriends. Anger was tucked away for women, sometimes
without our even knowing until it erupted from the dormant

cells it had taken up residence in. This is a tale of the suppressed anger that found a release in spite of my greatest efforts to keep it suppressed.

"Teetering on bitter" is how I'd describe my demeanor these days. What I'm learning is that it was never anger that was the enemy but misdirected anger, repressed anger that chipped away at my strength until well into my forties. World events stirred the fury pot with a giant ladle, leaving me twisted with an inconsolable rage that invited me into exploring a healthier relationship with the emotion I spent most of my life avoiding like the plague.

Anger is an emotion that I believed would get in the way of my mission as a Care Bear, so my body had to take the wheel and redirect my codependent mission to one that prioritized balance and self-care rather than martyrdom. It's been a long road . . .

* * *

ACCIDENTS 1 AND 2

I was sixteen, learning to drive on my mom's white, five-speed Honda Accord, when I backed into a shopping cart, scraping up the side door in a grocery store parking lot. My first boyfriend, Angelo, an Italian from Howard Beach, Queens, rushed to my rescue with an offer to bring my mom's car to "a guy he knows." To paint as accurate a description as possible, this was my first love. He was a short, angry man with a widow's peak who did really cool things like burn his cars for insurance money or get arrested for reckless driving. *And* he regularly impersonated the comedian Andrew Dice Clay, which made him oh-so-endearing—"Bada bing bada boom!" He drove us to the body shop in my mom's car, me in the passenger side with my generously hair-sprayed bangs at attention. I spotted a man precariously stumbling along the median between the eight-lane divided highway. My imaginary brake didn't slow down my testosterone-filled boyfriend. I felt my body tensing up, and before I could find the words to slow him down, I was stunned by the impact. The memory of the pedestrian crashing into the windshield as he rolled over the car, tufts of hair mixed with blood in the cracks of the glass, is one that will forever be etched in my mind. I opened the passenger door to find him unconscious and face down with his head lying in a pool of blood.

The man lived, but not without severe brain damage. It was shocking and traumatic. I was seventeen, and on some level, I knew that if I was driving, that accident never would have happened. I knew he'd kept his foot on the gas when he should have had his foot on the brake, and this might be the first time I've admitted that to myself or anyone else. I knew it meant my mom could lose her house if the lawsuit couldn't settle through the insurance company. I knew his reaction to what happened was callous. While the accident released a mosaic of feelings, it also solidified some in ways that wouldn't serve me over the years—the most significant early experience of abandoning myself in service of seeking validation from a man.

* * *

ACCIDENT 3

Walking from the subway on a rainy night in Manhattan after a waitressing shift serving burgers at Jackson Hole on the Upper East Side, I began to cross over Park Avenue. Jolted, a man in an SUV made a right on red, barreling into me and forcing my umbrella up and away as my body levitated and dropped to the ground a few feet away.

"I'm fine," I said. I made sure the man who hit me didn't feel bad. He was from California. He didn't know it was illegal to make a right on red.

"Do you want to go to the hospital?" asked the police officer as he tried to lead me away before I released the driver of all liability. I declined. I'd be fine. He made me wait in the back seat of his patrol car to keep me away from the driver. I don't remember if I walked back to my dorm room, took a cab, or was dropped off by an officer, but I found my way back to the dorm, lucid enough to call my mom and report the events of the evening. I was nonchalant and unconcerned. Once my mom consulted with my sisters, it was decided that I must go to the hospital to make sure there weren't internal injuries that would cause me to bleed out. I remember the hospital visit being underwhelming. I don't remember where it was. I don't remember what tests they did. I know there were no serious injuries, but the familiar post-accident, whiplash-induced headaches were a reminder of times past. What I do remember is that being the start of a growing number of random medical bills that would eventually make their way to collections.

I was at a low place at that time in my life, having been severely depressed for some years now. My self-worth was at an all-time low. I felt I didn't belong, at school or in a city where people had to wear such thick armor, where a chubby and sensitive girl better toughen up if she wanted to survive her environment. Things were bleak, but in a way, the accident enlivened me. Something was stirring in me—a sense of pride for being able to keep getting hit and get back up. Metaphorically, it shifted something. If I couldn't be angry, I could be strong.

* * *

ACCIDENTS 4 AND 5

An undiagnosed Epstein-Barr virus flare-up had been ignited by the breakup with Angelo. The fatigue was debilitating and made driving a challenge. It made a number of things challenging. I was known to fall asleep on strangers' shoulders on the train and miss my stop, get reprimanded at work for napping in meetings, and even need to record my college lectures because I could never stay awake for them.

One morning, while driving on the Long Island Expressway, I woke up to stopped traffic while going seventy miles per hour. Thankfully, the person in front of me was not injured by the impact of my car. I was, however. The automatic seat belt in that 1990 Dodge Colt was a literal lifesaver, but the injuries to my ribs, neck, and back would create the conditions for chronic pain for many years following. The ambulance didn't know if anything was broken, so I was carefully placed on a stretcher and put into the back for a trip to the hospital. En route, ashamed by what had just happened, I felt another jolt—a car plowing into the back of the ambulance I had been so gently placed in. After they moved me to another ambulance, I made my way to the hospital, where I was x-rayed and released hours later, denying follow-up care. Something that stands out about that day is the shame that overcame me as the EMTs had to lift my larger body from one stretcher to another. I'm not sure if they actually commented on my weight or if my self-hatred and internalized fatphobia conjured the words up on their own, assigning them to the EMTs. Regardless, I felt I was taking up too much space. I was sorry for the attention I required and did my best to not be a nuisance to the folks tending to my injuries.

This was just a hiccup, I told myself. It wouldn't stop me from leaving my hometown to seek a new life in California. I might not be able to follow through with the plan to use my just-paid-off Dodge to take my friend and me on a trip across the country, but we found a way to get there via train, hitchhiking, and bus. The money from the totaled car funded my road trip. My excitement for this epic journey out of my childhood sorrow to the land of milk and honey distracted me from the pain of the accident and may have even fueled my commitment to moving forward and onward.

* * *

ACCIDENT 6

Rear-ended by a tractor-trailer while taking a rescue cat back to the shelter, I was certain that it was a direct karmic response to having given up on the animal I had promised to care for. I don't even know how long I had the cat, but I do remember that she went nuts for McDonald's French fries. To be fair, Hannah was getting aggressive and unruly, and I was being forced to move out of the San Francisco studio apartment I shared with a friend. It didn't matter; I felt awful. Not only was I betraying this cat I had promised to be a guardian for but the transport was traumatizing, and I knew I wasn't setting her up for success when her feline post-traumatic stress response was to turn the volume way up on her aggression, prompting the shelter intake person to tell me that she would most likely be euthanized.

It wasn't until after this accident that I discovered a bodyworker to support my physical recovery. The gift of this accident was that I started to recognize that strength didn't come from abandoning myself.

SITTING WITH ANGER

∧∧∧∧∧∧∧∧∧∧∧∧∧

CAROLINA LASSO

I'M SITTING CROSS-LEGGED ON MY CUSHION, ATTEMPTING THE half lotus pose I've been practicing lately, eyes closed, hands on my lap, palms facing upward—a symbol of being open to receive. My intention for this meditation practice is to open up to connecting with my anger, an emotion that I rarely experience. Though I appreciate not using anger to create reactive, emotionally charged actions that I may later regret, I also know that, like any other emotion, it conveys wise information. I know anger has a place and a time and it can be helpful to set boundaries or to signal that something is wrong. I want to create a space to explore my relationship with this frequently-talked-about emotion and uncover why it's not so present in my life.

A few minutes pass, and I'm able to relax and momentarily let go of my thoughts. Rather quickly, I arrive at that familiar, blissful, and placid state that years of mindfulness practice take me to. Stillness, silence, serenity, and calm . . . are abruptly interrupted by a sudden realization that I'm not here for that purpose. With confidence, I guide myself, mentally saying the exact same words I use when I lead the emotional intelligence program I'm certified to teach: *Relax and now try to connect with that part in your body where you feel anger most intensely.*

A few more minutes go by with no clear end result. *Focus a little more and conjure up the feeling of anger*, I say to myself with an encouraging, academic tone. But nothing follows. No tingling physical sensations. No tension. No activation in any body part.

"This can't be right," I say out loud, breaking the silence in my room and changing my zen facial expression into a confused frown. *Anger is a universal emotion that* anyone *can replicate. I'm the emotional intelligence teacher here, how is it possible that I can't find my own anger?* I continue to think, losing patience and completely getting out of my meditative state.

Failing to accomplish the task sparks my curiosity even more. *Wait a sec, is* this *anger? Nope. It's frustration mixed with a dose of impatience and some confusion. I'm not there yet, but nice try!* I guide myself to mentally scan my most recent emotionally charged events and label the emotions I feel: *Disappointment. Sadness. Joy. Annoyance. Discontent. Anxiety. Gratitude. Frustration. Shame. Excitement.* All of those emotional experiences feel real and examples for each one of them quickly pop up in my mind and travel through my body.

Keep going back in time, perhaps there's a childhood memory or event that is blocking your anger, I now say to myself, reconnecting with my patience and sounding exactly like the therapist on a Netflix series I'm watching. Mental photos of my upbringing in Colombia pass through my mind quite rapidly. In a country where emotions are expressed with big hand gestures, loud voices, and revealing facial expressions, I see the images of people around me in angry, heavy situations and notice my aversion to that strong "negative" emotion. Memories from childhood point to the fact that I prefer serenity and harmony over conflict, and definitely over expressions of anger. There's an image of my parents having a heated argument, which my seven-year-old self dislikes to witness. Decisively, I throw a tantrum, distract them, and accomplish my mission: the anger in the room subsides. Peace is restored, and I go back to my Play-Doh.

Ok, we're getting closer. There's clearly something there about my relationship with anger. Keep looking, I urge myself mentally, continuing to guide my journey as if I were two different people—teacher and student. I travel forward in time to my school life. Images of the twelve years spent attending an all-girls Catholic school in Bogotá show up in my mind, bringing up many different types of emotions: anxiety when preparing for an exam; excruciating shame the day I wet my PE shorts because I was too shy to ask the teacher for permission to go to the bathroom; happiness (mixed with embarrassment) when receiving the best student award many years in a row; joy when receiving dozens of gifts at my first communion; disappointment (for weeks!) after making the mistake that prevented me from winning first place at a spelling bee; glee, amusement, and cheerfulness when connecting with my friends during class or over recess; frustration when receiving the imperfect score of 9.6 instead of 10 on a project; curiosity and interest when learning a new topic; sadness when my best friend leaves our school; and empowerment when going to the streets to protest a national affair, representing my school wearing my dark blue uniform.

As I can't find explicit examples of anger, I move forward in time to when I am seventeen. I see myself crying inside a bathroom stall in high school. I have just moved from

Colombia to Damascus, Maryland, where I don't know anyone. I don't speak English well, and I can't relate to the new culture I find myself in. I'm the only non-white immigrant in my class, and I feel excluded, different, and rejected. Not being able to fit in and belong fills me with sadness and confusion. It's the first time in my life that I realize that my skin color means something to other people. My cheeks are red, my hands are cold, my eyes are full of tears, and there's a hole in the pit of my stomach. I don't understand what's happening, and I don't want to be there. I want to hide. Despair. Homesickness. *Saudade . . .* that Portuguese word I recently learned. I'm not angry with anyone about my situation, not even myself, because I can't fully comprehend what's going on. I just feel small, confused, different, and powerless. Anger isn't here.

How about exploring anger in relationships? Better yet, romantic relationships? I bet thinking about men in my life will do the trick, I say mentally, unwilling to give up and even more curious to continue with my self-inquiry into an emotion I haven't really spent time exploring in the past. The day he, the one I thought would be "the one," breaks up with me, comes to my mind. I'm devastated. It's four months before our wedding day, and every detail is planned for the special day. My white dress is hanging in the farthest corner of my small closet and all 110 invitations are sent. My brother's best friend, my next-door neighbor for years, my parents' good friends' son, the perfect man on paper, my soon-to-be husband, decides to leave for another country for good without looking back. I see my twenty-four-year-old self crying on my bed, numb, confused, frozen, powerless. I am unable to be angry at him or hate him for leaving me. I still love him, even in the midst of his heart-breaking decision. Instead of blaming him, I feel guilty of perhaps not doing enough. I once again feel impotent. I don't eat much for a few days, I feel something dead inside me. I can barely make myself go to work. I'm filled with sadness, emptiness, a void, grief.

After many weeks of crying and feeling desolate, one morning, I hear a song that awakens me with a jolt of empowerment. Filled with new strength, and a willingness to redo my life without him, I decide to quit my job, apply to business school, and move to build a new life in New York City. The spectrum of emotions in this situation goes from frozen, numb, confused, sad, desolate, heartbroken, and indifferent to empowered and purposeful. Anger was never present in that episode either.

I think of the next decade and focus on my many other breakups in chronological order, all of which I initiated. Focusing on the endings of those relationships, I see tears, long embraces, good-bye letters, photographs, apologies, and broken hearts. I then arrive at my wedding day and quickly fast forward to the afternoon, three years later, when we decided to separate. I play that episode in my mind in slow-motion, carefully sensing the emotions that are present as two souls decide to take different paths. I don't feel guilt, and I don't blame him either. I don't feel small or devastated. I know it's the right decision. I feel sad, lonely, and empty, but hopeful about what will be next for each of us. I find myself feeling surprised and profoundly touched to see the beginning of a divorce filled with so much love and respect. Certainly no anger is here; there aren't hard feelings at all.

As I begin to close the chapter on my romantic relationships, my mind suddenly travels to a different type of interpersonal encounter, the times when men approached me or touched me in uninvited and inappropriate ways. My immediate reaction is to think of something else right away. Yet, I kindly encourage myself to open that door, take a peek inside that dark room, pause to sense how I feel, notice my sense of safety and readiness, and slowly follow one step with another, walking inside. With my eyes closed, I mentally see those faces, those scenes, and those hands crossing boundaries. I see myself feeling lucky for being able to escape every single one of those situations without major consequences—*unlike so many other women*, I think to myself.

Instead of focusing on the details of what happened, I invite myself to bring my attention to the emotions I feel in the middle of those events. I notice fear mixed with confusion, which doesn't allow me to think clearly. I see myself trying to find the right words and the right actions to quickly get out of each situation unharmed. In all cases, I play it cool; pretend I'm calm; and come up with an excuse, a reason, an explanation to get out of the situation. With a pounding heart, confused mind, and wet palms, my mouth moves, saying something that, indeed, gets me out. And after I do, I feel distrust, disappointment, and regret, usually followed by *I should know better!* And without having to deal with any major consequences, I do my best to brush it off, move on, and pretend it never happened. I move the scene to the dark room.

As I remember those events, I don't see anger present in my earnest self; the one who lived through them isn't angry. She is young, innocent, naive, and mainly doesn't know what is or isn't appropriate or what constitutes as aggression. She thinks of women who "really" experience abuse daily and decides her experience isn't comparable. So, she prefers to minimize it all through avoidance and silence. She locks the door and moves on.

Even though I notice the absence of anger in that young, confused, and innocent woman, I begin to notice my present self moving toward it. *There it is indeed.* Jaw clenched, toes curled, faster heartbeat, heat growing all throughout my body, a jolt of energy filling my limbs, tight chest: *I am angry.*

There are so many reasons why revisiting those experiences makes me angry, mad, upset, irritated, irked, indignant, or outraged. And as I go through that list of emotions, I sense an internal door opens the floodgate of other situations that elicit similar feelings—immigrant children, mostly of my own ethnicity, being separated from their families at the southern US border; politicians changing laws that remove or reduce women's rights; the military killing innocent young boys and girls in my native country; the violent invasion of many people's lands; human rights being violated in so many corners of the world. That anger quickly becomes impotence, which feeds the anger and then dissolves into resignation, disappointment, and paralysis.

Still sitting with my eyes closed, sensing such a wide range of emotions and finally being able to connect with my anger, I arrive at a few insights. First, I realize how long it takes me to connect with my anger and how it's not often present in my daily life. Perhaps due to my upbringing or my own strong conflict-avoidant personality, anger clearly isn't an emotion I feel frequently. While it may be seen as something positive, not expressing my anger has prevented me from setting boundaries and clearly articulating to others when something is not ok.

Indeed, people close to me have mentioned that it is often difficult for them to know if something bothers me. Anger is an emotion most people understand fairly clearly: if Joe expresses anger, Jane understands that something is wrong, and they take action. Its absence or repression may prevent communication in many circumstances. I remember that my current partner tells me that I often "skip" anger and quickly move into disappointment or indifference. He shares that he would often prefer to see a clearer expression of emotions rather than the difficult-to-understand silent mode that I often move into. He wants to have a deeper understanding of the emotions I'm feeling, no matter what they are. I also want to deepen our connection through the full range of emotions that may be present and more clearly articulate what I'm going through. I know that takes time, but I'm willing to work on it.

My second insight is that my anger is short-lived, and it rarely stays for too long. When I feel anger, I notice that it rapidly turns into another, deeper emotion. This realization reminds me of a paragraph from Brené Brown's book *Atlas of the Heart*:

> When research participants talked about being angry, the story never stopped there. Their narratives of anger unfolded into stories of betrayal, fear, grief, injustice, shame, vulnerability, and other emotions . . . . The more data we collected, including interviews with more than fifteen hundred therapists and counselors, the more certain I became that anger is a secondary or "indicator" emotion that can mask or make us unaware of other feelings. . ."

---

11 Brené Brown, *Atlas of the Heart: Mapping Meaningful Connection and the Language of Human Experience*. (New York: Random House, 2021), 221.

According to Dr. Brown's research, it may be easier for people to express anger instead of a deeper emotion, either because of language limitations or because it's easier to use the label "anger" than something that exposes our vulnerability. In my case, perhaps as a result of my emotional intelligence and mindfulness training, it's the opposite: I'm more comfortable going into a deeper emotion than anger. There's usually an underlying, more powerful experience that takes over or that is more clear to me than anger.

And my third and most powerful insight is that when I feel angry, it's usually related to a high degree of injustice or a human rights violation. This is an area I'd certainly like to explore further. I'd like to know how to use my anger as a potential catalyst for change. I want to harness my strong emotions as inner messengers of what's not right, of what's not aligned with my values, of the causes I'd like to fight for, and to set boundaries in my own life.

With the clarity of these insights, I feel a sense of completion. I remember that all emotions bring along wisdom with them. I am reminded that emotions visit us temporarily; they come and go. Instead of rejecting them, avoiding them, or fueling them, all we need to do is sit with them, gather the insights they may be trying to convey, let them pass, and take action with new information. As I bring my practice to a close, I realize how much depth there is to my relationship with the emotion of anger. I know I'm far from done with this inquiry, but I feel gratitude for the wisdom received. I take a deep breath and open my eyes.

THE UNSAID WE CARRY

CHLOE ROWSHANI

T HE WORD "TRAUMA" NEVER SAT QUITE RIGHT WITH ME. IN therapy sessions, it was easy to call my father Narcissist and my mother Echo. Naming the way they were behaving helped me understand that I was only human for feeling so fucked up all the time.

I had only ever associated trauma with really horrific and isolated incidents that ravaged the mind, body, and spirit—a car crash, sexual abuse, a soldier in live combat. My parents didn't touch me or hit me. Others knew them to be not only kind but also charming. My mother's laugh would raise the spirits of any room, and my father's confident demeanor always made you want to lean in to learn something new.

But when it was just us, the energy was starkly different. Our house felt less like a home and more like a prison. My father would widen his eyes really big to scare my younger brother and me out of eating too slowly or laughing too loudly. As early as primary school, when I couldn't figure out a math problem on my own, he'd ask me to get up and bang my head on the wall to see if the answer would come to me that way. I'd cry loud enough to avoid hurting myself and instead be dismissed to my bedroom. I hated my mother for not asking him to stop his scare tactics, knowing somewhere, deep down, that I didn't have to just accept living in fear.

My mother's only fault wasn't her passiveness in the face of my father's terror. Unlike my relationship with my father, where we consistently moved between power and fear, with my mother, every day was different. One moment, we were best friends, interlocking arms, giddily trying whatever new treat was selling at the mall while we dreamt up our next escape. The next, she was so upset by something I did or said that she'd coldly proclaim that she no longer loved me and that I was no longer her daughter. I'd spend days, sometimes weeks, attempting to reclaim her love, sending my apologies and love letters through our messenger, my younger brother.

My parents made each other worse more than they made each other better. It still boggles my mind that my father looks back on their times together with such fond memories because I don't really remember those at all. I don't remember them ever having a good time together unless there were drinks involved or friends around. At home, they could either be found spending time in separate rooms or fighting in the same one. At any moment, the wrong tone of voice or a contradictory desire could set one on the other's throat or, worse, ours.

I don't claim to have the best memory. If anything, I claim to have one of the worst out there. Even so, is it really my fault that all I can recall are the memories I don't want to remember? The screams and shouts, the cops showing up after worried neighbors phoned in, the packed suitcase waiting at the foot of the door. I'd instinctually hide away with my brother, cupping his ears, trying to distract him from the scene unfolding in the other room. I wanted to protect him in the ways I wished someone else was there to protect me.

My mother never honored my attempts to keep myself and my brother unharmed by all that we couldn't control. She'd barge into our hiding places with bloodshot eyes, dragging my father in with her, demanding that I choose who I loved more. I don't recall ever answering the question, knowing even at the age of six that there was no right answer. I could see how my hesitance to respond chipped away at my mother's ability to trust me. In their worlds, someone was always right and someone was always wrong. Someone was loved and someone wasn't. Someone was good and someone had to be bad.

By the time I hit double digits, I was both the victim and perpetrator of nearly every limited belief pattern. I ruminated on the narrative that I was an inherently bad human with only good moments, writing in my journal one day that I was as worthless as a defective toy on a production line and on the next writing that I hoped my future resembled that of the ugly duckling's. I didn't want to be alone, and yet, I felt safest when I was, laying on the cold, green tiles of my bathroom, holding space for myself in the only room with a door that could be locked.

My father's inherited fear of scarcity and inability to trust anyone instilled within me an anxiety-ridden drive to be the best so that, ironically, I could hopefully one day set myself free from needing to be anything other than myself. You would think a cancer diagnosis would have changed our perspective about the way we lived, but it didn't. My mother was forty-three when she fearfully sat across from her doctor alone and learned that she had stage three breast cancer; I was twelve. She was still dreaming of what life could be;

I was just beginning to dream. Even before the news, I was plotting ways to save us from our present lives. After her diagnosis, that mission became more dire.

I believed for the longest time that, with my help, my mother would muster the strength to leave my father and begin again. I thought that the vote of confidence I gave her to leave was enough to inspire a change. But cancer seemed to put all of that on pause, scaring my mother into a paralyzing fear that if she died, her children would be both motherless and fatherless.

I quickly learned how to swallow my emotions so that I didn't contribute further to her pain. I'd shame myself into staying home instead of asking if I could go on ride bikes with my neighborhood friends because I didn't want her to feel like I was choosing them over her. I learned how to cry without making a sound, getting so good at it that I could cry in the most exposed places—during a classroom activity, at a birthday party, at the communal benches during snack time.

For eight years, my mother's cancer came and went and came and went, slowly and painfully spreading. While, together, we collectively continued to deny the possibility of her dying, I thought about it all the time, visualizing all of the potential ways that I would be told she was no longer with us. I didn't ever get to just be a kid. While my friends' greatest worries were their school crushes, I felt like I was cracking under the weight of trying to save the version of my mother that hadn't yet been given a chance to fully come alive.

I began to have a very short fuse. Everything that didn't go according to the plans in my head set me off like a firecracker. I wanted to fight. I wanted to hurt others so that they could share in my pain. I found a sick comfort in learning that I could overpower my parents by dangling my suicidal ideations over their head. I felt like I was screaming, "Love me! Protect me! Save me!" and no one could really hear it. The summer before I began high school, I timidly confronted my mother, simply telling her that something was terribly wrong with me, unable to put any of my other thoughts into comprehensible words. That's when my journey with therapy began.

In the beginning, it felt incredibly awkward to be asked to open up to a stranger about thoughts I had never articulated to anyone before and revealing a side of my parents that nearly no one outside of our home had ever seen. After a handful of sessions, my thoughts spilled out of me like a waterfall, sometimes muddled with painful sobbing that fell out with it. Those four walls and my therapist's notepad held all of my truths; for once, I felt seen. It felt good until it didn't.

At first, when my mother would pick me up after sessions, I'd share everything, both of us feeling a sense of relief from having our feelings about my father validated through me. A few months in, though, I began to have a harder time sharing when I realized she, too, was a part of the problem. It became more clear that, even if unintentional, she was hurting me just as much as my father was. All I wanted to do was scream at her to "Wake up and be an adult. Do something to save us!" Instead, she'd ask about our sessions, and I'd sit there in silence, unnerving her with my secrets.

However fucked up it may seem now, I felt a sense of freedom when my mother passed away. I could live my life on my own terms without feeling guilty about leaving her alone in the desperate life we shared. As an adult, every day was a chance for her to choose a different path forward. As her dependent, I counted down the days until I was eighteen and could be on my own. I tried running away a few times, but I never got very far, afraid I'd encounter worse on the streets than what I was dealing with at home. But the attempt to leave always felt cathartic. There was power in sending a message that if you fucked me up too much, I could leave and live.

It took nearly a decade after her passing to finally claim my experience as trauma. Part of that journey included learning how to hold space for my anger. In my childhood, there wasn't ever any room or patience for it. Only my mother and father were allowed to be angry, show anger, and be angered by life. They couldn't handle it in others though. Even tamer emotions, like frustration, weren't tolerated.

Instead of learning how to be angry, I became really good at being sad. Sad for others, sad for myself, sad for my sadness. I've become somewhat of an expert at navigating my life and feeling an ever-steady presence of sorrow. I'm a landlord that's accepted sadness as a squatter, coming to appreciate its long-standing presence as a reminder of my resilience despite all of its unseen weight that I carry.

I do wish I knew how to carry anger similarly. Today, if someone is angry with me, I either cry and want to run away or I offensively laugh out loud. If I allow my own anger to just be, to just show up in all its rawness, it comes out as an unintelligible scramble of words relayed in a loud and condescending voice, similar in tone to my father and similar in coldness to my mother. I hate everything about it.

I don't want to be any of the bad parts of my parents, and I despise that so much of my brief and precious time on earth has been spent trying to learn and unlearn all that's been imparted on my subconscious. My parents weren't all bad; no human is. If anything, to be human is to be a whole of many, many intricate parts. Even knowing that to be true and cherishing that fact as a beautiful wrinkle of life, I still wish both my mother and father could have realized the damage they were causing before the damage was done.

I'm not sure if, how, or when I'll ever share any of this with my father. I don't think he'd ever be able to handle a truth that's so different from his own memories. If I ever did, I'd also have to prepare myself for the possibility that I could be hurt further by not only his denial but, worse, his disparagement. What's still heart-shattering, though, is knowing that I'll never have the chance to share any of this with my mother. I want to believe that if she had lived long enough to survive, one of us would have saved both of us, and the lives we continued to share with one another would've been completely different. In that alternate reality, we would've held space for one another in ways we never did when we had the chance.

Through my trauma and my grief, I've come to learn that life is just a field of landmines with triggers everywhere. One day, I can feel a sense of normalcy, grounded in the present, secure in all that I carry, and the very next day, something trivial could send me back to what feels like ground zero. I've asked myself the same damn existential questions about my life and my memories over and over again as if I have never asked and answered them before. I always return to the same conclusion: either I allow the things I carry to control me, or I allow the things I carry to co-exist.

Coexistence is a brutally challenging endeavor. I've found that if you let your guard down, there's a high chance you can get hurt. It takes a fiercely intentional discipline to be aware of what's showing up at any given moment. I imagine the secret of living is being able to walk through that field of landmines, fully knowing that the next trigger could destroy you, and still choosing to make the journey.

It's a beautiful visual. It's what I envision people mean when they refer to the Buddha's way. I really want to believe that there are people who have actually achieved that type of nirvana, but I'm still extremely skeptical. How can you be okay knowing that all you're carrying is weighing you down from really living? I'll be pissed about that for life.

CONVERSATIONS
WITH ANGER

∧∨∧∨∧∨∧∨∧∨∧∨∧∨∧∨

CHRYSTAL BELL

I HADN'T ALWAYS SEEN THE ROLE OF ANGER IN MY LIFE AS BEING akin to a relationship. Relationships were between people and certainly didn't include those threads between me and my own emotions. I knew my anger as something that often hid in the shadows but could also be wielded to get me out of a bad situation (it never worked). In my endeavors to be "good" and avoid the anger of others, I did things I didn't want to do, said things I didn't believe, and stayed silent when I could have spoken. I avoided anger, centering the comfort of others at the expense of my own values. There were even times when I used anger as a means of escape. In my twenties, I ended a couple of romantic relationships by making my partners so angry that we split up. I used anger to create an exit strategy because I didn't otherwise have the courage and skills to say I wanted out. As long as there was anger between us, I figured I could insulate myself from the heartbreak of ending those relationships, but all it did was compound the loss and cause deep hurt.

As I've moved throughout my life, I've accepted my anger, naming the intricacies of my relationship with it, learning from it, and honoring it. Through this, I come home to the parts of me that experience and encounter this force and energy every day as part of this humanscape to which I belong.

Anger has made me turn over the soils of my past, exca-vating layers of memories in order to understand it. In order to truly know my anger, I return to the fires that forged it.

My first lesson about anger was that it was to be avoided. As a small child, I watched my mother's frequent anger from the shadows, so often fueled by delusions. I saw anger as a reaction to something that was not real, and the symptom of the thing that pulled us apart. During my elementary school years, when I lived with my grandparents, I watched their anger weaponized against one another in frequent arguments and discord, the air so tense it could cut. I longed for peace and stillness. On the inside, I made myself small, hid within my own imagination in a place where anger didn't exist. On the outside, I would become silent and still, my face without expression, waiting for calm to come again. I didn't want to be like them. To me, anger equaled chaos. I needed order, so I organized my things until they were tidy, arranged, and aligned. I craved emotional control and reason, even prided myself in it. I learned to fear my own anger and quiet it inside. I chewed on it; held it against my tongue; and worked it into a small, manageable disappearing thing to find refuge from the wars, real and imaginary, raging around me.

Anger is a guide, leading me down a path of exploring my identity, with all of its history, contexts, and things I have control over and things I don't.

Leaving home for college as a young adult allowed me to feel my own limits and edges. I began to explore what I was willing to endure and what needed to be pushed back against. I started to see the larger contours of anger in the world through my own Black, queer, woman body. I studied resistance movements, marched in the streets at protests, listened to freedom songs, joined affinity groups, ate fire with the Lesbian Avengers, read Audre Lorde, and felt my father's civil rights-era involvement in the Black Panther Party like a life force in my blood. This awakening helped me reconnect the severed parts of my own emotional landscape. What was once something to be feared became a source of power and resistance. Anger became a tool of survival by providing purpose, providing energy, and calling me to action. I cannot exist in this world, living in this body, without being connected to my anger.

Anger is a reminder of distant places, exposing old ways of being and whispering in my ear to be gentle with myself. I put my fears aside and trace the throughlines back, letting those memories wash over me.

In childhood, avoiding the dangerous, uncertain landscape of emotions felt like the safest place to be. I worked this skill like a muscle, adding grief, heartache, and love, among others, to the list of emotions too complicated to embrace. Back then, I couldn't see the toll it was taking on me, the growing dissonance between what I felt on the inside and how I appeared on the outside. It made me anxious until I became so accustomed to turning away from the feeling that I became numb and lost my own sense of self. In the rearview mirror, I see that I misunderstood anger. I didn't know how intimately connected it was to the things that really mattered to me. As an adult, I have looked back with sorrow, regret, and even shame at those early times when I could have used anger to stand up for myself, to protect what I loved. I'd been too willing to sacrifice a piece of myself for an unsteady and unworthy peace. My young self could not yet see how powerful it could be or how powerful *I* could be. I didn't know that my ability to feel and express anger was what allowed me to feel more whole. Even now, from a wiser place, I can still feel the way that early education works on me and in me. Sometimes, I still feel the pull to shrink in the face of anger.

Anger illuminates the power of observation and inquiry. When I can get perspective on the source of my anger and ask questions about it, I honor it and become wiser in the face of it.

I watch and feel my anger shape-shift, evolving as I get older and with circumstances. As my own capacity to be with anger becomes larger, I'm asked to dive deeper and be closer to it; to move in it, around it, through it; and feel it move in me, around me, and through me. From this place, I can be curious about anger: *Where do I feel it in my body? What is it doing for me? What would it be like to let it go? What would it say about me if I could let it go?* I follow an inward road of accepting the parts of me that used to oppose this challenging emotion.

Anger reconnects me with my body, sometimes feeling its heat, other times touching the things beneath it—grief and deep sorrow. When I feel anger that is stuck in my body for too long, I am reminded that something more may be required.

I've learned about anger by doing it, by being angry, by letting something move and shake me enough to experience it in its many forms. I can be outraged, furious, livid, or just plain mad. Once I slow down enough to feel it in my body, I examine why I feel angry. I hold it, work with it, let it move me to action, or let it dissipate on its own. In that sense, I've come to trust my anger, trust that my body will know what needs to be done. The more I feel it as embodied energy, the more I'm able to understand it. The point is rarely for me to simply get rid of the anger, but rather to feel it, its roots, its impacts, and how it inhabits my body. From this place, release and movement become possible. Sometimes, when the initial searing hot moments are over, I can just be with what is beneath the surface. Anger becomes the doorway to access the pieces of me that simply hurt.

Anger also reminds me that it must be tended, sometimes with motion, as a countermeasure to soften what has become rigid and immovable.

* * *

I walk through the forest for a conversation with anger. Although it has been nearly two years since the incident, I want to believe that I left it behind in that difficult phone conversation. My body, however, is telling me otherwise. The heat from it is still with me as though it had just happened. I feel it, hot in my chest and behind my eyes. It twists its way around my tongue, not wanting to let it go. I feel tightness, place my hands over my heart, feeling its grip, and, I walk this way for a long time, stepping over fallen branches, smelling the thick pine of the trees around me. My anger has served its purpose. I begin to imagine myself without it . . .

I pick up a heavy splintered tree limb from the ground, nearly too large for me to carry and so unwieldy that I cannot swing it through the air. It is just enough for me to raise it above my head and allow gravity and rage to slam it to the ground in front of me. The first blow sends reverberations singing through my body from the impact. I lift it again, and the second thud comes down harder, sending the loosened dirt shooting into the air. I feel every blow dislodging the fury that ravages my bones. The limb splits: one becomes two, becomes three, then four. My whole body is heaving at the effort, and I breathe the damp forest air more deeply. Somewhere in those blows, a large sliver of wood breaks off, exposing the inner layers of the limb. I pick it up, examining the wet, longitudinal sections, as though a knife has deeply whittled it away. How strange it is to see this beautiful segment broken off. I consider taking it away with me to dry for a future ceremonial burn. But like this anger, I want to put it to rest right now. I cannot imagine holding onto this thing, beautiful as it is, for a second longer than I have to. I kneel in front of the nearby tree and give that piece of wood up as an offering. It's that old anger that leads me into the forest, and I want so badly to leave it here so I can return, restored, more empty than when I arrived.

* * *

Anger is a force that has the power to keep me grounded in what matters to me. I am most myself when I am oriented toward my purpose, my deepest longings, and the things I imagine for myself and the world I am helping create for my children.

In 2020, during America's long overdue and temporary moment of so-called "racial reckoning," I was an executive in a law enforcement agency. Although I'd spent nearly twenty years there, nothing prepared me for what work would be like against the backdrop of national outrage and protests—the same elements that felt so alive in me. Nothing prepared me for the silence I was greeted with within the halls of police headquarters in the wake of George Floyd's murder. Few of my colleagues understood what I was experiencing; for many of them, it was as though it was just another day. As the sparks of the first few days were igniting, so did the anger inside me. I watched as businesses, organizations, and even law enforcement agencies released statements of support for Black lives and denounced the events that had taken place in Minneapolis. In my mind, their words felt hollow, inadequate, and not at all enough to make up for the harm they were complicit in or responsible for inflicting. Anger helped set me on the path of redefining how I wanted to spend my life, my mind, and my energy. I radically changed my direction, eventually leaving public safety in pursuit of alignment and a deeper calling.

Processing my anger requires me to communicate. Whether it's who I am angry with, who is angry with me, or just the quiet noticing of the feelings within me, anger is a conversation that is most fruitful when I'm willing to have it.

This is the part of anger that feels the riskiest to me, standing in the face of fury or having done or felt something that caused harm and responding with the words and actions that feel at scale with it. Communicating anger can call for instant action, or it may mean sitting with it, holding it long enough to find the right words so they can be delivered and received in the ways they are intended. I notice the places in my life where my tendency to sit with it first has dampened the energy in an unhelpful way. And I also see where that same response has salvaged relationships and reminded me that they were worth saving. I have experienced the peculiar intimacy that comes from having been deeply angry at a person and having worked through those feelings, knowing that it is possible to have felt the gamut of emotions toward someone and still love them and be willing to go forth with them in spite of it all.

What I notice the most at this time in my life is that anger continues to teach me and call me to action. Just when I think I can predict its course and outcomes, I find that something in me has shifted just enough that I'm caught off balance, uncomfortable once again. I arrive at places, some unfamiliar, others so old and deep they feel ancestral, carrying my anger with me, finding my way as I feel my way to how I'll respond to what feelings are evoked in me, the way I'll communicate. Ever connected to the threads of my past, anger continues to pull me to something new and evolving.

THE LITTLE ENGINE THAT JUST DOESN'T

∧∧∧∧∧∧∧∧∧

DULCEY REITER

Y OU KNOW WHAT MAKES ME ANGRY? WELL, THERE'S A LONG list, but I'm on it. I make me angry.

In spite of being a highly functional adult (most of the time), I still often struggle with feeling inadequate. Inadequate in the sense that I am Sisyphus reincarnated (granted, my "boulders up the hill" are *much* less sexy mountains of laundry and to-do lists) and that I, too, am destined to never succeed at the task at hand.

In spite of daily attempts to put my best foot forward and be whatever the best version of myself is that day, I have this sense that I always fall short of getting done what I mean to do—and, (very) unreasonably, what I do manage is just about never enough—which too readily translates to believing that I'm somehow not enough. And this, of course, is garbage. Though, this feeling of ineptitude coats me like tarnish and leaves me so angry that I cannot seem to redirect my course.

I feel like a marginally better-dressed version of Charlie Brown (replace the yellow shirt with a red hoodie) going in to kick the football and landing flat on my back, staring at clouds—always trying, never quite pulling it off. There are days and weeks that I'm so many different flavors of failure, I could just about serve them out in waffle cones with sprinkles. And this sense that I'm failing—in so many ways, on so many days—leaves me with a slow burn of anger that I am, in fact, inept, while knowing full well that this cognitive distortion is not an accurate take on reality.

I can make a pretty compelling case for my status as a functional adult: I haven't lived with my parents in decades; I pay bills, meal plan, and budget; I schedule vacations; I hold a job; I dress myself every morning; and I feed the kids (hey, *and* the cat!) with the best of them. I even remember to water the houseplants most of the time. I do all the things that should make me a card-carrying member of the Adequate Enough Club. And to the casual observer, I would appear to be a solid member. Logically, anyways, I *am* a member.

Maybe.

The Struggle
Being a parent.

I aspire to be an easy-going parent who really gets and appreciates that my kids are little and, as such, are highly prone to acting like little kids. This means knowing and being prepared to work alongside creatures who will not a.) always listen; b.) do what I politely ask (and more often are compelled to do the opposite); or c.) hey, acknowledge my existence. I get it. And I recognize that this behavior isn't personal and is pretty standard operating procedure for little beings who are figuring out the world and who don't have fully developed prefrontal cortexes. Yet, there are moments when my inability to navigate my interactions with my kids as a functional adult makes me want to throw my own tantrums.

Despite how I mean to show up in the world, my frustration in asking a kid for the eleventh time to deposit her insanely dirty socks into the laundry hamper can make me suddenly turn into a toddler myself: forgetting my inside voice; having utterly irrational expectations; and no longer having an ability to process the world as a calm, self-soothing adult ought to. It's not my most endearing trait. In fact, it feels like plain old failure in the moments when my kids are making me nuts *and* I have completely lost my sense of humor, ability to creatively problem-solve the chaos at hand, and capability to put some healthy distance between my emotional state and the situation.[12]

And, sure, we're all human—imperfect, a bit inconsistent, and required to make peace with experiencing a side of ourselves we struggle to accept—but the contours of a pattern I see repeating make it hard to feel like I could be considered anything but inadequate in these moments, and it's hard to rewrite the script.

I'm not managing this well. Again. Why am I not doing better this time? This isn't who I want to be. And then I feel angry at myself for getting it wrong yet again. And *then* I'm also angry for getting angry at myself, because what does that accomplish? Suddenly, it's a messier place to reside in my head with this layer cake of anger baking in my thoughts. I recognize the need to give latitude and accept I won't always get it right, but this well-established, repeated pattern of missing the mark on parenting feels so formidable it might as well call itself plaid.

---

12 Not to mention all the other parenting fails, including adorning my kids in a sundry of unwashed lost-and-found items I dug out of a box at the pool for having failed to pack everything but their swimsuits for swim lessons.

Being a Partner

Once upon a time, I was a thoughtful, caring spouse who had my own independent life, interesting thoughts, and clear ambitions for what I wanted to achieve professionally. And while much of that's shelved in a box somewhere in the back of a closet with kids on the scene, it feels like yet more proof of how much I cannot manage to do, even though I observe other functional adults around me pulling this off, seemingly with ease. The jerks.

I have become a cardboard cut-out version of my previous self. I am someone that now thinks in literal to-do lists, whose gambit in most conversations is about what needs doing (because what spouse doesn't love an intimate conversation that starts with, "Did you take out the trash?" or "Is the litter box clean?"). I'm also not entirely sure what direction I'm heading in life or what I even find fulfilling. I'm still in the shadows, eclipsed by the demands of parenting and still navigating the murky oceans of who I am now. I seem to have lost what makes me tick, leaving me utterly vexed that I'm not showing up in my relationship as the thoughtful, interesting person I knew myself to once be.

Being a Professional

To find oneself suddenly trying on middle-aged for size (it's still a bit loose, but apparently, it's one-size fits all) but somehow without the "mid-career" title to match is less freeing than it looks. It's unsettling. I find a lot of my energy consumed by still navigating a career trajectory that looks like a line drawn by my three-year-old. It hasn't been made better by two years of a pandemic, and in my worst moments, it leaves me feeling like a failed professional who's still uncertain about what steps to take next.

Presumably, our worth, value, and identity are not defined by our careers. *I* know this. *You* know this. (We hope everyone else knows this.) But it weighs. It weighs me down some days almost physically, as though someone dialed up Earth's gravity, and I'm doing all I can to stay upright.

I've spent great swaths of my life getting degrees and working unpaid internships, followed by a montage of various nonprofit jobs with an unwavering desire to help change the world for the better. And yet, I still find myself wondering what I'll actually be when I grow up.

With the usual things that come with professional tumult—dysfunctional work environments; unfulfilling roles; the difficult dichotomy of work versus family; and, more recently, the challenges of parenting through a pandemic—I struggle to deflect the anger I direct at myself for not having figured out a more stable career trajectory earlier in life than at the confluence of circumstances that leave me still standing awash in professional uncertainty. And while I'm by no means a unique snowflake in the nationwide chainsaw juggling act that is balancing parenting and a career in the US, in my own myopic story, I'm the common denominator here. Surely that must mean *something* about the role I play in all this? Surely it's . . . me?

The Case for Adequate

To think of oneself as "inadequate" isn't the happiest frame of mind through which to view the world. To *know* that being inadequate is actually an unfair, incorrect assessment, and to still proceed to *feel* inadequate is, well, rather maddening. I clearly see the cognitive dissonance, though I feel as though, somewhere on the path to becoming a parent and navigating a once-in-a-lifetime pandemic, I've lost my

footing and ability to recognize that, while we may not succeed in everything, this does not translate into failure. It's so
basic on its surface and somehow so much harder to internalize. This is the fuel igniting my anger. How is it that I feel
so unraveled by something I logically understand isn't a fair
or accurate reality of my day-to-day? When did this tarnish
of ineptitude start to seep so deeply into my thinking, and
how have I lost the ability to frame how I think about it?

I have spent years traveling to far-off places, navigating
unknown terrains, cultures, and languages (plus a handful of dicey situations . . .) and have come away from each
of these with not only a deep appreciation for the vibrant,
complex world we live in but also a deeper appreciation for—
and understanding of—myself and what I'm capable of. I
remember a mosaic of moments that gifted me with a sense
of feeling both competent and complete in the world, where
languages, cultures, and life experiences weren't barriers
to connecting: Slinging my backpack over my shoulder as
I boarded the next train to Whoknowswhere, Europe. The
lively "conversations" expressed solely through hand gestures and pictures drawn in my spiral ring notebook with my
host family in Thailand at age sixteen. Braving the mosqui-
tos on the porch of a bungalow in Bali to play Yahtzee with
newly made friends from all over the world. I've been there,
and, in fact, have done that.

There's little that compares with getting out of your comfort zone and finding the flexibility and creativity needed to
navigate any situation to really lay bare who you are and
what you're truly capable of. And in spite of this clear evi-
dence that when the situation calls for it, I can and do rise
to the occasion, it's still, bizarrely, a struggle to feel like I
haven't rewritten the script that proclaims I'm failing at life.

For me, one of the starkest reminders of how capable I am stems from a moment in my life when I had to reckon with how close I came to losing it. About a decade ago, I awoke from a deep haze and noticed my parents sitting sideways on the wall through my fuzzy vision. It took me a few beats to register my world perspective lying on a hospital bed as the disembodied voice of an ER nurse behind me explained that I'd been in a serious bicycle accident five days prior and was being woken now so they could extubate me. After the listing of my extensive injuries, which included several missing teeth (eleven, to be exact), missing pieces of my nose and lips, deep lacerations on my face as well as my tongue, and a few broken bones in my hand, amongst other injuries, I spent a few moments taking in what this all meant for this new life I was waking up to. It was . . . a lot to take in.

While there was no way of knowing at that moment—or maybe even accepting—that my road to recovery would last the next five years and include eight intense surgeries (two of which lasted six hours), ten procedures that included tattoo laser removal on my face to remove the trackwork of purple asphalt railroaded across my face, and too many appointments to count (though surely in the hundreds?), I figured this all out bit by bit.

And, rather curiously, it was in the throes of recovering from my traumatic accident that I found myself in possession of a self-awareness I never knew was possible. Everything at that moment in my life was a struggle—eating, showering, getting myself dressed, going for a walk around the block with such limited energy—but my ability to tune into just how I was feeling, understand it, and move on felt like my super strength at the time. In spite of a face so broken that people would actively avoid being near me in public on more than one occasion, I had never felt so whole or capable of appreciating my life.

Somehow, at a moment when I was also in such a vulnerable place, living on my own without a lot of family nearby, facing a recovery process I didn't yet understand the extent of, and heading for bankruptcy in order to bankroll surgeries that were neither "medical" nor "dental" according to American health insurance providers (and, consequently, being forced to pay out of pocket), I felt not only competent but very whole.

I felt whole at that moment in my life thanks to a crystalline gratitude that I not only survived my accident but that I was expected to make a reasonable recovery that wouldn't leave me enduring chronic pain for the rest of my life. Defying death and pain, given the circumstances of my accident, left me genuinely elated to be alive. I also felt strength in my complete acceptance of what had happened to me—and to my appearance. Being able to look at my trauma-damaged face without judgment of my appearance—for perhaps one of the first and only times in my adult life—was also immensely freeing. It's one of the few moments in my life I had no internal critic, because I had made a conscious choice to focus on healing and discarded anything that did not serve this purpose. I also felt deeply lucky to have survived such an ordeal and grateful for my life.

And it's worth mentioning that I also had a community of people supporting me, some of whom I barely knew or had never met and who were touched by what I'd been through. It was so humbling and comforting to be so cared for in a moment when I truly needed it. This experience gave me the ability to really distill the measure of my life into what mattered: being alive, being grateful, and being in a community.

And, Yet

And yet, a decade on from such a dramatic moment of personal tumult, I find myself happily married to a unicorn (ok, a human, actually, but a unicorn, nonetheless), raising two thriving, ridiculous kids in a comfortable home . . . raging against this feeling of inadequacy that I cannot seem to mute. It's baffling.

And, while I'm embarrassed by and want to swat away my own delicate, porcelain-like fragility in all this, the truth is that it's also debilitating. My brain feels divided into two uncooperative halves: the half that intellectually understands all that I'm capable of (as a member of the Adequate Enough club) and my inherent self-worth and the emotional half that doesn't ever quite seem to believe what I know to be real, leaving me with a gossamer of inadequacy I can't ever seem to brush off.

No to-do list is ever finished; what I do manage all too often feels insufficient, and I don't have a sense of any forward motion at this moment in my life. I can't figure out if I lack ambition or direction on where to jump back into the fray, but I'm no clearer on my next professional steps than I was as a largely clueless college graduate. I'm always trying my best, aiming to embrace a learner's mentality, and striving to be a better person but often wonder if it'd be any different if I weren't putting concerted effort into trying to improve and move forward.

It's hard to place this sense of self-doubt and stagnation in the larger context of what's happening both in my life, caring for family, and in the world at large. Instead, I internalize these shortcomings or missed goals as a personal failing, and it makes me flustered that I cannot do more. I then feel even more anger toward myself for being so unreasonable when I'd never think such a thing of others. I'm exhausted from grappling with this undercurrent of not-enoughness.

I know this struggle is not unique and that I'm not alone in these struggles of feeling inadequate.

It's a strange juxtaposition to consider how my physical and financial brokenness left me feeling so strong mentally at one moment in my life, and—now that my body has recovered and I have, in so many ways, just about everything I ever thought to hope for in life—I feel so lacking.

And while at this moment in my life when I'm angry about feeling the constant, exhausting struggle of "figuring it all out"—my identity, how I want to show up in life, and what direction I'm headed—I hope to find my way back to a place where I can distill all the noise clanking in my thoughts down to what really matters. The obvious answer seems to be to focus on the obvious: being alive, being grateful, and being in a community. And while these things aren't the missing piece of the puzzle that'll make everything better, perhaps it's a starting point from which to inch back to feeling whole(r) again, or at least less angry about it all.

And while there's no escaping life's Sisyphean towel-folding or dinner-making tasks, I'm hopeful I can get myself off my long list of things that make me angry.

NAVIGATING ANGER

∧∧∧∧∧∧∧∧∧∧∧∧∧∧∧∧∧∧∧∧

HIDEKO ANDERSON

F OR ME, ANGER FEELS SO PERSONAL, SO VISCERAL, IT'S HARD
to put into words and explain old stories of anger because
it's just something I feel in my body. It's something that feels
overpowering; sometimes it can feel scary, and other times it
can feel liberating to express and move through.

My anger feels like it originates from a place of fear. This
fear forks into two different roads—a road of distress and anxiety and a road of annoyance and outrage. The second road
leads to anger, and this road is made up of layers. The first
layer is my fear—my fear of the unknown, my fear of change,
and my fear of not having control. The second layer links
these fears to my core wounds of perfectionism, people-pleasing, and a sense of worthiness. Over the past few years of
exploring my fears and wounds, I can see clearly where and
when my anger first developed.

For most of my life, I have felt like a victim of anger and
tried my best to hide it. I remember being told as a little girl
not to cry because it made me look weak and vulnerable. I was
told not to make a scene or call attention to myself by having
a temper tantrum. These ways of being led me to understand
that it wasn't okay to stand out—survival meant fitting in and

not making a commotion. I learned to "not be difficult," to get along with everyone, and to be well-liked. I did that by following social cues and maintaining an extremely laid-back and agreeable persona. I ensured that the people around me felt comfortable. I could feel when people would tense up over a confrontation or disagreement. As a child, I quickly felt the embarrassment of my mom if I acted out publicly. She would pull me aside and reprimand me, and we would leave the store. I, too, became embarrassed by being openly scolded and learned to adjust my behavior. I yearned for the validation and praise for "not acting out."

Over time, this guided me to lack boundaries and become a supreme people pleaser. When I couldn't meet someone's needs or expectations, the feeling of disappointment in myself and failure overshadowed my own thoughts. The self-loathing and victim mentality directed anger at me for not doing something "the right way." On the other hand, if I did meet someone's expectations and needs, but they didn't reciprocate, a feeling of not having control of the matter led to anger directed outwardly toward others.

I dreaded when the teacher would take attendance in grade school; kids would tease and taunt me because my name was "funny." I was furious that kids and teachers alike couldn't learn to pronounce it when I had taken the time to learn theirs. I was even more upset that my parents had given me this name, something completely out of my control. I demanded to go by a simpler name for the majority of my life to avoid the ridicule. I can vividly remember how anger felt inside me—a tight chest, an explosion of fire in my heart, and a feeling of uncontrollable rage coursing through my veins.

As I got older, lacking boundaries and people-pleasing eventually led me to burn out in jobs and toxic relationships.

I would sacrifice my needs to prove myself in jobs: In the restaurant industry, I was pressured into taking extra shifts because they were short-staffed. I would opt not to take breaks because it was too busy, and I would volunteer to run to the store to get supplies while using my car and gas to show how dedicated I was. In relationships, I naively supported partners who didn't keep their word and routinely ghosted me only to show up days or months later. I would welcome them back because I hoped for better and wanted to prove I was worthy of their love.

I found myself questioning why I routinely ended up in these places time and time again. What was holding me back? My fear of change, my fear of the unknown. I was scared to do something new and not know the outcome. What if I failed? What if people didn't like me? What if I wasn't smart enough? What if I wasn't good enough? These are the types of anxious questions flooding my brain on a regular basis, and I suppose they engulf many women's psyches.

How do women navigate anger? Carefully. With such balance and calculated precision that it makes me dizzy trying to comprehend how unfair it is for women.

Women have to carry the burden of navigating our anger in such a way that is deemed proper and inoffensive to the rest of society. I feel I can't express my emotions openly because it traps me in the stereotypes that I'm either soft-spoken and weak, crazy, or an overly emotional bitch. This perception—that women need to adhere to the social norms of perfection, of being a "good girl"—is so invasive that a lot of us perpetuate it without conscious awareness of its insidiousness. By over-apologizing, by not speaking assertively or directly, by hiding or wiping away our tears, we hide the undesired show of emotions, including anger, to appease others. We have become conditioned to aim for agreeability and perfection, to ask for permission for something that we know our body or mental health needs.

I have developed this need for perfectionism, because if my speech, my project, or my task isn't done perfectly, it will be because I'm a woman. The pressure I feel now to deliver these stories is deeply uncomfortable because my perfectionism and unworthiness come forward. I gaslight myself into thinking my experiences aren't good enough to share. The truth is, there isn't one cringy story to share as an example; it's an accumulation of multiple experiences and microaggressions from men and women throughout my life that have made me feel this way.

Furthermore, identifying as an Asian woman deepens the complexities. I'm categorized into the stereotypes of being a bad driver, a math prodigy, a submissive and obedient woman to men, and an embodiment of the model minority. If I can't live up to these standards, people are confused and direct microaggressions toward me: "We had the Asian girl on our team—we should have gotten that answer right!" "Wow, you're actually pretty good at driving. I'm surprised."

These are comments I've heard too many times throughout my life. Getting caught in this loop of trying to fit in but not meeting societal expectations angers me. I feel trapped and out of control again.

Wanting to get out of this loop and make sense of the rage and frustrations, I feel a need to talk about my emotions more. I began slowly and somewhat unconsciously a journey with myself, starting to excavate my past layers to uncover that I actually had a lot of anger bottled up inside. Upon deep reflection; journaling; and discussing with friends, family, and mental health guides, I kept hearing the same question: "Are these fears and wounds yours?"

I thought, *Of course they are, I've developed them over the years and through my experiences of interacting with people.* Moving out of my childhood home, living on my own, and then returning home to interact with my parents, I began to notice similarities in how they processed emotions. I was able to see that my parents modeled a lot of these behaviors, thoughts, and coping mechanisms, which is how I learned them. I got it from them, and they got it from their parents.

I knew my parent's history, but peeling back the layers of assimilation and survival is different for each generation. I formed the basis of my relationship with anger, and I was given the tools to navigate it in the only way my parents knew how. Both were true. Realizing the roots of my Japanese American ancestry, connecting the dots to my grandparents trying to stay safe in America after World War II, I understood why the energetics of people-pleasing and a lack of worthiness came so easily to me. The fears of the unknown and not having control made sense to me after understanding what my family and past generations had gone through. The concept of perfectionism also resonated with maintaining the status quo of the model minority and not giving anyone a reason to question my existence.

My mom was scared of being different, never wanting to cause a scene or draw attention. I can vividly remember the sounds of her getting ready every morning while I snuck into her bed and pretended to sleep. The sound of her lipstick opening made a plastic pop along with the noise of an aerosol mist. The fragrant smells of hairspray and perfume flooded the room as she continued getting ready. She always put her makeup on in the morning and had a matching pair of stockings and underwear. She would say, "Just in case something happens, I want to be put together." You could say she was vain, but I believe her reputation and that of her family were hugely important to her. She didn't want anyone to associate her not dressing well or looking a certain way with the reputation of her family.

I have come to an age of maturation where knowing what runs me, both ancestrally through my lineage and also through societal programming, gives me awareness—awareness of what is really at the root of my anger. With that awareness, I have a choice to continue this way of being or try something new that's better aligned with my current values and environment.

With the opportunity of choice, I wanted to change my situation. My situation was a place of despair in my late twenties, where I wasn't happy and felt like a victim of my circumstances. I had ended a three-year, unhealthy relationship and was uninspired and trapped in my low-paying, nonprofit job. I felt depleted. I didn't consciously know at the time that my specific relationship with anger wasn't working for me or had even led me to this place. For the majority of my life, I had hidden behind my anger and chosen to play it safe to make others around me feel comfortable. I was starting to realize my way of being with anger was taught to me, passed down through generations. Sick of feeling like a victim to the anger, I craved a new path, but like many young adults, I didn't know how to cultivate it on my own. I wanted a blueprint—someone to show me a healthier way to navigate my anger, uphold boundaries, and practice self-care. I decided to take a leap of faith and change my circumstances.

Spoiler alert: there's no blueprint. I knew I had to get uncomfortable by doing things I wouldn't normally do and find out what I really needed to thrive. For me, moving to a new city and cutting ties with toxic jobs and relationships was the catalyst to start a new foundation that was authentic to me. It wasn't easy to leave a place where I lived close to everyone I'd always known; my fear of change was constantly front and center.

I cried about letting go of furniture, clothes, and material items while I packed up my things to move. These were items that had no sentimental value—another pattern that had been passed down from my parents and grandparents. In my family, material items symbolized success and a level of comfort in owning numerous possessions. It was also an element of feeling prepared for any given situation. I could hear both my parents saying, "Keep this, you might need it one day." Again, having that awareness was helpful in maneuvering through these transitions. Like the anger, it wasn't unique to me, instead, it was a familial pattern. It was also deeply emotional for me to say goodbye to my parents, brothers, and friends who knew me so well. I wanted to keep holding on to the same dynamics of staying in the loop as if I still lived there, but I knew that was preventing me from being fully present in my new home.

Navigating new jobs and new relationships, I had the opportunity to practice speaking up and honoring my needs. I started feeling more confident, each time improving my self-worth by incorporating what I was and wasn't going to stand for. By getting more comfortable negotiating the salary and terms for each new job I started, practicing saying "no," and confronting housemates about dirty dishes, my boundaries started to firm up. And there are plenty of times when I easily slipped into my people-pleasing ways by working too much, not asking for what I wanted, and burning out of jobs and relationships again. Each time, I became more aware of the missteps and reflected on how I could approach these situations differently in the future. I'm slowly but surely creating my own blueprint of self-empowerment and values.

My relationship with anger is still very much a work in progress, and I'm accepting that it will always be expanding and contracting. Evolving and flowing as I enter new phases of my life, it's being met and tested along the way. As much as I want it to be a skill I master and move on from, I know that's still my perfectionism coming up and societal influence dictating that emotions and states of mind can be neatly packed away. Currently, I have been deeply working on cultivating my own knowing, building upon my knowledge, and strengthening my propensity to listen to my intuition. I have many of my own experiences to start forming opinions and a level of discernment to connect and evolve my inner wisdom of how I want to interact with the world and what it throws my way.

Admittedly, I still have a tendency, a craving, to look to other people to show me how to process my anger, my fears, and my wounds. By acknowledging that this is usually my go-to reaction of wanting to fit in and "do it right," I can come back to myself and try to discern what's true for me. My fears of the unknown, of change, and not having control are still present, but they have lessened their grip on me because I have the awareness to not fight them and to accept that these fears are woven into my DNA. I have come to understand that these fears come from my lineage out of necessity and served a purpose to survive in an environment and time that demanded it. I realize that this isn't my reality, and I have the privilege to choose another way. And the best way to honor my lineage and acknowledge my privilege is to act differently and continue to evolve my relationship with anger.

THE ANGER TRAP

KAT PEDERSEN

W HEN I WAS IN COLLEGE, THIS GUY STUCK HIS HAND IN MY burrito. No, that's not a euphemism. If you'll stop snickering for a moment, I'll explain. It was a dreary winter Saturday in 2004. I was at a rehearsal for some silly debutante performance, probably hungover, and everything was running late. Hours past lunch, I was super hungry, so a friend agreed to bring me a burrito from Chipotle.

When it finally arrived, I was elated. Enter asshole, stage left. For reasons unknown or long forgotten, he'd been picking on me for weeks. Today was no different. What's-his-name walked right over and stuck his entire hand into my burrito before I could take a bite. He wiggled his fingers, scattering rice to and fro, and then he walked away with an impish grin on his face.

Was he flirting with me? Was he trying to punish me for some unknown slight? Was he simply bored and looking for a laugh? I don't know, but I was stunned and disgusted. Even though I was famished, I couldn't bring myself to eat the mush that remained. I sat there for a few minutes, staring at the mess formerly known as my lunch. Then I walked into the other room and slapped him.

Obviously, the slap was a little dramatic. Writing this in the wake of Will Smith's "slap heard around the world," I'm tempted to cast an even more critical eye on my behavior, but I won't overthink it.[13] I was hangry, and also a little immature. To make matters worse, no one in the other room knew what he'd done, so I looked like a crazy bitch, and the decidedly more popular asshat proceeded to tell everyone I was a crazy bitch, which didn't help my case or reputation. And that, my friends, pretty much sums up my problem with anger: all my life, I've had no idea what to do with it, and everything I do seems to make things worse.

* * *

Like most women, I wasn't taught how to handle anger as a child. I realize now that most of us never received the emotional education we probably deserved, but in all fairness, our mothers and the generations before them probably didn't either. Women in our culture are supposed to be *nice*, which doesn't leave much room for disagreement or intense emotions. In my case, I wasn't allowed to be angry at all. This wasn't an explicit family rule, but I paid a hefty price any time I expressed inconvenient feelings, so I learned to suppress my emotions early on, and I've been doing it ever since. Here's the thing: You can only suppress anger for so long. Eventually, you're going to slap the jackass who ruined your lunch, and everyone will think you're the problem. It's the perfect anger trap. Damned if you do, damned if you don't.

Choosing the lesser of two evils, I've, therefore, spent much of my life trying *not* to be the problem, which basically

---

13 "Will Smith—Chris Rock slapping incident," Wikipedia, last modified January 29, 2022, https://en.wikipedia.org/wiki/Will_Smith%E2%80%93Chris_Rock_slapping_incident.

means I became an epic people pleaser. Any time I deviated from this path, the people around me—my family in particular—reinforced the idea of me as the problem, effectively shaming me back into place. Was it them? Was it me? Well, nothing is black and white. Yes, I needed to learn how to be assertive, but at the same time, they didn't want me changing in ways that might make them uncomfortable. This is common when people benefit from unhealthy relationship dynamics. However, I also adopted this story and saw it everywhere. I believed it, so I acted accordingly. To truly grow up, my story needed to change, but it would take a lot more learning, not to mention a lot more pain, before I was ready for that.

In the meantime, this dynamic propelled me to success in my professional life. I was well-liked, often promoted, and seriously overworked. For years, I rarely said "no," which made me everyone's favorite doormat. What's more, I rarely stood up for myself. Based on my previous experiences, I assumed it would make things worse, so I tolerated behavior that was, well, unacceptable. Companies love women like this, especially in the startup and tech industries. In my opinion, most of them want employees who give until it hurts and then keep giving, regardless of any abuse endured along the way. I just smiled my way through it, but inside, I was fuming, even if I rarely allowed myself to feel it.

I was like a tea kettle. I accepted whatever happened and ignored my feelings until the pressure became too much to bear. Then, I'd start to whistle, surprising myself and anyone who happened to be on the receiving end of my unexpected emotional outburst. It was rare but unpleasant for everyone involved. In fact, it was so rare that I still remember the moment I hit my limit with a dismissive team leader more than a decade ago. When another colleague emailed to reschedule a meeting a few minutes later, my response was short and rude. I felt terrible, but I didn't know how to make things right, so it showed up on my performance review months later. Once again, my hidden anger revealed my dirty little secret—I was the problem. From then on, I buried my anger even further, but anger has to go somewhere. Eventually, I started directing it at myself. This dynamic came to a head when I started a new job at one of the hottest startups in town.

I won't name names, but a lot of people would happily cut off a limb to work at this place. I just got lucky. It appeared to be my dream job, so I quickly fell into a routine of working day and night with only a short break on Saturday afternoons. I loved what I was doing, or so I kept telling myself, and I did it well, so they promoted me quickly. They celebrated my "hustle" while casually encouraging me to stay single. They repeatedly told me this was the key to my success. Something inside me felt sick every time I heard that, but I kept shoving down my feelings. No need to rock the boat.

Unfortunately, that wasn't the only red flag. The men who ran the company were larger than life and occasionally scared the heck out of me. One was all dapper suits and designer socks. At first, I thought he was an excellent people manager, but after months of strange situations and half-truths, I realized he was an expert people manipulator. Brilliant with a strong need to be adored, he often held court around his desk, and anyone who didn't swoon effectively enough quickly fell out of favor. I never found a way to speak his language, so I often felt like I was playing a game I couldn't win.

The other was equally brilliant but very different. He couldn't care less about appearances, so he wore workout shorts every day and played by his own rules. His bold nature and unconventional honesty drew people to him, but he had a dark side. Sometimes, he'd totally lose his shit. In other words, his eyes bulged, and he screamed until the walls shook. His fury had the force of a hurricane that could tear a person down, both physically and emotionally. I know because, even though he's been an incredible mentor, I was a frequent target of his outbursts. Whenever the storm hit, I turned into a puddle of tears, but I never fought back. I just took it, and it tore me apart.

Between the two of them, I was constantly walking on eggshells. Yes, I was terrified of provoking the one who raged, but my rocky relationship with the other caused me far more anxiety, and hidden under that anxiety was plenty of my own rage. Did I ever express it? Of course not. I barely let myself feel it because I was convinced something bad would happen if I did. After all, everyone else could see what these men were doing, and no one else seemed to have a problem with it, or so I thought at the time. Clearly, that meant I was the problem, once again, so I suppressed my emotions until my body took over.

In the words of Gabor Maté, my body started saying "no" very clearly.[14] Within nine months of joining the company, I was having trouble walking and using my hands. My joints were swollen—red and aching as if I'd been beaten—but doctors couldn't find a reason for my pain. Remember how I said people would happily give up a limb to work at this place? Well, I was on the verge of losing multiple limbs, and I definitely wasn't happy about it. Eventually, I was

---

14 "When the Body Says No: The Cost of Hidden Stress," Dr. Gabor Maté, accessed June 30, 2022, https://drgabormate.com/book/when-the-body-says-no/.

diagnosed with rheumatoid arthritis (RA), a painful auto-immune disease that causes extreme fatigue, swollen joints, and other challenges as the body destroys its own connective tissue. Some people believe it's caused by unexpressed anger that gets trapped in the body. In other words, I was so busy suppressing my anger that my body created a debilitating condition to get my attention. Ouch.

Despite all of the pain I was experiencing, I kept hobbling back to work for almost a year until I finally reached my breaking point. Once I left, my RA symptoms improved immediately, but I had more work to do. Intuitively, I knew I had to find a way out of this anger trap. I couldn't keep repeating this pattern, so I set off on the most intense healing journey of my life. Things got worse before they got better, but as I worked through some of my childhood trauma and dealt with the stories that were keeping me stuck, I felt better. Slowly, I learned to appreciate my anger. It was trying to help me. In a way, my worst fears had come true. I was the problem because I was allowing these things to happen to me, but that meant I was also the solution, and my anger was showing me exactly what I needed to do.

* * *

I don't remember feeling much anger as a child. When I was in elementary school, I remember my parents spanking me whenever I did something that made them angry. I feel a vague sense of unfairness when I think about it, but I was a powerless child then, so there was no point in dwelling on any anger I may have felt. What could I do about it? Later, I remember my father raging down the hall, his face red and his fists raised. My stepmother begged me not to provoke him. Some days, I ignored her, but she was always right. It wasn't worth it. In our family, he was allowed to be angry; I was not. If I showed anger, I would be punished.

Now, I'm old enough to see the double standard, but in my innocence, I learned the wrong lessons. I learned I was bad for showing or even feeling anger. I learned people would leave. I learned men could scream, or do much worse, and women were expected to just take it. Specifically, I learned that *my* anger only made things worse, so I found other ways to cope. I can feel compassion for myself now. I did what I had to do as a kid; I just wish I'd known I didn't have to carry that story and those coping mechanisms with me into adulthood.

As an adult, I'm no longer powerless. I didn't have to slap burrito boy, though he certainly deserved it. I could've calmly told him his behavior was unacceptable, or I could've avoided him altogether. In fact, if I'd addressed his bullying weeks before he ruined my lunch, the whole incident could've been avoided. We teach people how to treat us, and I taught him it was okay to pick on me.

I also could've stood up to family and friends who had called me the problem over the years. If I'd stood my ground, most of them would've come around eventually. And if they weren't willing to accept my boundaries and treat me better, they would have left. In that case, good riddance. We all deserve to be surrounded by people who love us and treat us with respect. (The latter is not optional.) My behavior was only a problem when I exploded or when I expressed anger in unhealthy ways, but it's perfectly acceptable to calmly and clearly share that you're feeling angry. It's easier said than done sometimes, but it's become something I aspire to because I can't suppress my emotions anymore. My body won't let me, and my body is wise.

Finally, was that work situation the one-sided mess I thought it was? Was I completely powerless? No. Did those leaders have some issues? Probably. Was one of them struggling with his own anger? Absolutely. If anyone can understand that, I can. Or at least I can now. In my case, I had to learn that I was allowing them to treat me that way. I gave more than I wanted to give, and I tolerated treatment that I consider unacceptable, but it was all my choice. It was also my responsibility to say "no." That's what my anger was trying to tell me the whole time. It was sending me a message: *Set a boundary. This doesn't feel good. Please don't allow this. I love you.*

I'm not sure I love my anger yet, but I understand it better now. It doesn't take over because I don't ignore it anymore. Sometimes, I still want to slap someone, but I don't. Instead, I spend time with my anger when it appears. I'm getting to know it. I take it slow, let it simmer. I ask questions. I tell it I understand, that it makes sense. Then, once my body has released most of the charge, I try something new. Sometimes, I share my anger and make a request. Sometimes, I set a boundary. I don't always do it skillfully, but I no longer feel like the problem, nor do I believe I'm bad for feeling anger. Even when my feelings or actions trigger others, I'm okay. At this point, I know that logically, but it doesn't always feel that way. I'm working on it.

For now, I've let myself out of the anger trap, and I'm discovering a world of possibilities. Some feel good, and others don't. I'm starting to think there are a thousand healthy ways to handle anger and still maintain loving relationships. Similarly, there are a million ways to be a good woman who's doing her best. I'm a woman who feels great anger sometimes, even if I don't always know what to do with it, even if I'm still figuring it all out, and even if there are things in this world I can't change. And there are plenty of things for women to be angry about right now. Maybe that's nothing new . . .

Experiencing this much anger can be deeply uncomfortable, but a part of me believes there's great power in anger. The more I tap into that power, the stronger I feel. The more I accept my anger, the healthier I get. Even though doctors said it was impossible, my RA symptoms are disappearing. I'm determined to keep healing until it's in remission, and my anger is the key to this miracle. If I listen to my anger, maybe my body won't need RA to get my attention anymore. If I learn to love my anger, maybe it'll share its secrets. Maybe anger is my greatest ally and my greatest teacher.

TALKING BEHIND SOMEBODY'S BACK

∧∨∧∨∧∨∧∨∧∨∧∨∧∨∧∨

KATIE KARLSON

W HEN I WAS IN MIDDLE SCHOOL, PEOPLE AT MY SCHOOL didn't include me in a lot of things. I wanted to know what everyone was talking about, but every time I asked, people said, "Oh, it's just nothing." I wanted to be friends with all those people because they seemed cool. They bullied me about my age and even called me dumb sometimes, but every time I told them to stop talking badly about me behind my back, they didn't. Thinking back on it now, why would I want to be friends with those people?

IT'S NOT SKIN CANCER

∧∧∧∧∧∧∧∧∧∧∧∧

LEXI LIGHTWOOD

"**S**TOP DRAWING ON YOUR ARM; YOU'RE GOING TO GET SKIN cancer."

Reluctantly, I put the pen away. I bring the sleeve of my jacket up to my palm, covering the fresh ink on my skin.

It's 11:30 a.m, halfway through design class. It's the second time today and the fourth time this week I've been told I'm going to get skin cancer because I draw on myself.

* * *

"I'd date Lexi."

I'm talking with my friends Rebecca and Alice when the conversation shifts to whether or not we'd date any of our friends. My two friends start talking about how they've known each other forever and wouldn't date each other. We've all known each other for eight years. We were in the same first and second-grade classes.

"I'd date Lexi," Rebecca says to me. Alice nods, and maybe it's jokingly, but my heart grows a little warmer.

I'm pretty sure Rebecca has a crush on me because they always hint about us dating. And I'm in a fake relationship with Alice in the hopes of driving off my classmate Bob, who's been stalking me. I have a real girlfriend, Hailee, but I'm pretty sure Bob thinks she doesn't exist.

* * *

"Why are you scratching yourself?"

"It's just a bug bite," I lie.

Scratching myself is my form of self-harm. By scratching myself, I am putting enough force into something I will feel, but it won't leave a scar. I can do it whenever I need to. Sometimes I'll scratch myself with a pencil when I want to feel more pain, but that only happens when I "mess up," or what I call messing up. If I say something weird, or talk too loudly, or feel like I'm not being myself, that's when I scratch myself with a pencil.

But no one at school knows that. If they did, the teachers would be watching me 24/7, making sure I wasn't doing it, which would just make it worse. That's why I lie and say it's a bug bite. That way, no one can rat me out. That way, I can have peace.

* * *

"Why do you draw on your arm? You're going to get ink poisoning from doing that constantly."

I'm talking to Belle, and again, I'm being told I'm going to get a skin disease. Do I care? No. Is it her skin? Also no. Did she look up how dangerous pen ink is? Probably not. So why does she care if I draw on my arm?

* * *

"I can't tell the difference between a friend and a crush."

Let's say there are two people, Sean and Maia. Sean is your significant other, and Maia is your friend. When you're around Sean, you're allowed to randomly hug him, allowed to kiss him, allowed to do whatever it is you two do when you're alone. When you're with Maia, you're allowed to randomly hug her and talk about whatever you want. But you're not allowed to kiss her or cuddle her because that's not what friends do. You're not supposed to want to kiss her, because she's your friend (and because you have a boyfriend). But then why do you want to kiss her and cuddle her, too? And not just her but everyone—all of your friends, your coworkers, and even your family. That's how I feel. And if I feel that way about everyone, then do I like everyone or no one?

This makes friendships really difficult for me because I don't know if I've had a crush on all of my friends or none of them.

* * *

"Go kill yourself."

I'm playing a videogame with my cousins, and that comment, even though it's meant lightly and in the context of the videogame, still strikes me, cold and hard like a blade you use to cut meat.

They mean I should die in the game, not in real life, but that doesn't matter. They still said it.

* * *

"That could be seen as borderline self-harm."

My design teacher is talking to me. I put the pencil down. He continues helping the student beside me, and I pick it back up again. I use it to scratch harder at my arm, trying to draw blood. It doesn't. Instead, it makes angry red spots that look like a rash.

"Can I go get water?" I ask the teacher. He nods, and I get up and walk out of the classroom. I don't need water, but I do need a break from that classroom. Being in there makes me feel like I'm going to simultaneously pass out, have a panic attack, and kill myself. And the bright lights of the classroom and the loud noises of my classmates are leading me to feel hyperstimulated.

* * *

"You all right?" My dad walks by me. I nod, keeping my eyes closed.

My eyes are wet with tears that aren't even there. I'm lying on the floor in the middle of the hall. I have both earbuds in, and for once, I feel at peace. I'm in my own head, creating stories that I wish would happen but know never will. This place in my head, though much darker than this world, is the only place I feel truly happy. Not the happiness you feel with your friends or with someone you haven't seen in a while but the true joy that emanates when you realize your dreams are possible.

I've only ever felt this joy in my stories and dreams and when I'm with Hailee, the only person I feel that I can trust, the only person who I know loves me as much as I love them.

* * *

"You're going to get cancer."

I just blew out a candle in my room. How am I going to get cancer from that? I whirl around to face my younger sister.

"Tell me," I say, anger boiling in my veins, "why am I going to get cancer?"

"It smells like smoke."

I want to roll my eyes and slam the door on her, but I don't.

"I opened the window. And you don't get cancer from breathing in smoke."

She has the decency not to argue back. "I'm just looking out for you. You might damage your lungs."

I want to tell her about my classmates who smoke, how they don't have cancer and they purposefully inhale smoke. Or how you get a cancer cell in your body every ninety seconds. But I don't. I know it would scare her. So, I keep my mouth shut. She walks away.

* * *

I expect too much from people. And yet, I should expect more. There should be someone who will be there; there should be someone I can talk to. About how I want to live and how every second here still hurts. I want someone I can trust.

* * *

"Well, what do you normally do when you're done eating?" My dad asks me during dinner.

"Feel bad about wasting food," I say, mostly to myself. I've just finished eating dinner. Well, what my dad says is finished. I'm only halfway done, but I feel full. I don't want to throw away the food because I'm training myself to eat everything on my plate—that way I don't not eat. But I can't eat anything else.

I stand up and throw it away. I want to cry to my dad, but he wouldn't understand.

* * *

"People don't commit suicide because they want to die. They do it because they don't want to feel pain anymore."

I try explaining this to my dad as we're sitting in the car.

I try telling him I need help. I try to find a way to explain what I feel. But he doesn't understand.

"It's part of being a kid," he says. "Everyone goes through that feeling."

I nod, pretending not to be listening so we can end this conversation.

There's a reason I don't tell people about my problems. They try to give me advice that won't work, but I don't need their advice. I just need someone who will give me an answer. Someone who will be able to label exactly what I feel and fix it. But that's not going to happen. The only person that can fix me is myself. And I can't do it.

* * *

I'm sitting in class, my hand raised, the answer to the question clear in my brain. I'm the only one with my hand raised. And then someone shouts out the answer. They get the answer wrong, but the teacher doesn't call on me.

Later, when I ask what the assignment is, he doesn't answer, so I ask again. No answer.

I'm so mad at him, and I want to shout out and tell him to answer the fucking question, but I don't. Instead, I grab a pencil from my bag and start drawing on my planner. It doesn't calm me down, so I start driving the pencil into my arm and leg. Then I break the pencil. I'm still not calm, but there's nothing else I can do.

I stay quiet and put in my earbuds. I want to kill him.

* * *

"There are many better people you deserve."

I curl my legs into my chest, using the rocking chair to move me forward and backward over and over again until

I can finally pick up the phone again.

I read through the whole thing this time. This message, the one I'd been dreading yet knew would happen from the beginning, Hailee has finally sent it.

I cry silently while I finish reading it.

"—it took me a while to realize I liked you back. And I liked you for a while. Over the summer we grew apart, and it's sad—"

Yeah, Hailee, it is sad. It's sad that the last memory I'll have of us together is of me being too nervous to kiss you again. It's sad that I'll never be able to find anyone like you no matter how hard I search. It's sad that the first time you held my hand, I knew we wouldn't be together forever, and yet I still choose to believe that we could be something.

"—I love your pretty little face and problem-solving skills. You are sensitive to your surroundings and care about others—"

If you really loved me, you'd still be with me. You wouldn't have sent this text about "growing apart" even though you said we could wait until high school if it didn't work out. Just admit it—you don't love me anymore. Don't come up with all these excuses to try and make me think we can still be friends after this.

"—platonically love you and you deserve much more than me. It's gonna be okay."

I'm crying so hard now that I'm surprised I'm able to stay quiet.

"Lexi, what do you think about—" My mom stops when she sees me. "Are you crying? What happened?"

I turn my face away. I don't want to tell her about this just yet. "I'm not crying. I was just rubbing my eyes because there was something in them."

She knows I'm lying, but she leaves my room anyway.

After a while, I finally respond to Hailee's text. I tell her I've been feeling the same way about her, that way she doesn't feel bad for breaking my heart.

But as the weeks pass, I realize I lied. I still love her, but she doesn't love me back anymore. And she never will.

* * *

Drive this car into the tree. End my life. I dare you.

The voice in my head, so strong it almost sounds real, dares my mom to drive us into the next passing tree. We're arguing, well, disagreeing—sort of. We aren't seeing eye-to-eye on something, so I'm getting yelled at. She doesn't take a breath long enough for me to interject. She calls my dad. He allows me to get a word in. But then I get yelled at again because that's "Not what you said when we were talking." Because she didn't let me get a word in. And "Wow. I can't believe y'all. You act differently around me than you do with your dad." That's because my dad allows me to get a word in. He allows me to say what I need to say. She never stops talking.

* * *

What the hell is wrong with you? You idiot, you fucking idiot. Nothing is wrong with you. You're just overreacting.

My nails dig into the skin of my arm, but I can't feel them. I claw at my neck. I punch my arm. I want the pain to go away. I walk across the room and grab the x-acto knife on my bookshelf. I take a block of rubber that's next to it and carve away, putting all my strength, all my energy, into scratching out a design.

The blade sinks into the rubber easily. I pretend it's my skin. I pretend I'm tearing away pieces of myself until I'm just a single atom. From there, I can rebuild myself. I can become the person I've always wanted to be.

I'm halfway done with my design when I stop.

Why aren't you crying? I ask myself. *Why aren't you sad?* I try explaining to myself that I'm trying to cry, that I'm trying to get the feelings out.

"Anger and sadness aren't the same thing," a voice in my head tells me, and I know it's true. I know I need to allow myself to be sad without wanting to hurt myself, but I can't. Not yet. I can't even let myself be sad.

* * *

"Stop talking!" I yell at my sister.

My mom makes me apologize, even though I don't feel bad. I haven't felt bad for a while. Every apology makes me realize this, because each time I say the words "I'm sorry," I immediately say after that I don't mean it. Some people say that, by doing that, I'm being mean. But I'm being honest. I don't lie to my friends or family. They always think I'm lying to them, but I'm not. Because if I believe what I say, that makes it true. Right? No, that doesn't make it right. I need to stop taking out my anger on other people. I have to learn to deal with it on my own.

And so, that's what I'm doing. I start finding ways to control my anger. I find ways to make it so I'm not going home and hiding in my room. I make it so the days are filled with good.

Eventually, I get the best day of my life:

"Wanna continue chatting?" Jay asks me.

I don't normally talk with him, not until recently at least. This is what I would consider our second real conversation. We're not talking about anything in particular, just random things to pass time. We walk around for a while until we have to go to class.

Later that day, I'm playing this game called wall ball. It's my first time playing, but I'm doing really well. I've won three times and am tied with someone else for second place.

After that, I'm sitting in Spanish class with one of my best friends. We're not really talking about anything, just listening to music and chilling with each other.

"If there is one thing you could change right now, what would it be?" she asks me. I think for a few seconds, but my mind fails to think of anything.

"I don't want to change anything," I say with a smile, "I'm really happy right now, and I don't want to change that."

She smiles, "You're really happy right now?"

"Yeah, my day was really good." I think back to walking around with Jay, playing wall ball, and now just sitting here in Spanish class. Today, I didn't need my scratching. Today, I didn't feel pain.

* * *

Now, don't get me wrong, I'm still mad at myself. Mad at how stupidly brilliant I am. Mad at how ugly and beautiful I am. Mad at how perfectly imperfect I am. Mad about how I don't overthink enough when overthinking. Mad about everything that makes me who I am. I know people who would kill to be blonde, or be a second degree black belt, or have as many friends as I do. Even the fact that I can solve math problems almost as easily as breathing could cause jealousy. I love who I am, and yet, I hate myself for not loving my personality more. But I'm figuring out how to deal with anger now. I can write stories, vent to my friends, and even occasionally channel it for sparring in martial arts.

And that's why I know everything will be okay. I know I'll be fine. I'm learning to live with my bad thoughts because, after all, they're just thoughts. And though my brain is powerful, even it has weaknesses. Don't worry, I'm not going to kill myself. The only thing that's taking me out of this life is either old age or skin cancer.

HARNESSING
THE DRAGON

LINDSEY KUGEL

IT STARTS LONG BEFORE ANY "TRIGGER." I FEEL STRESSED, AM running late, or am mildly irritated about something not going my way. Or it might be the general subconscious sense that I am not worthy of respect, and suddenly, confirmation bias is working against me . . . . Often, these moments build in interactions with my children, where the issue starts small and then gradually increasing offenses start to become untenable.

Then the moment comes—the kid says, "NO!" defiantly, or worse, starts incessantly whining about some near-nothing, usually something I can do nothing about. Parents—we've all been there, right? I try, in the most firm but understanding ways I can, to calm the situation. I seek to understand what's driving the behavior—"Why might she be like this? Is she just tired?" —starting from a place of compassion and holistic love. I listen while attempting to shut down the behavior. I am working my hardest to be the best mom I can be, to set strong rules but also allow them to be who they are.

This does not work. The tantrum continues, the behavior worsens, and the kid digs in her heels. Repeated attempts to stop the behavior, both calmly and then with more fierceness, fail. And then, all of a sudden, I've arrived at my wits' end. I can no longer stand for what's happening for a single second.

Then, I am pulling my daughter by the arm across the car into her seat. Or screaming in the face of my half-broken-hearted, half-bemused son, "Shut up! Not another Goddamn word!" Or hurling plastic toys and letting out a blood-curdling, monosyllabic shriek at the tantruming child on the other side of the bedroom door.

The anger has built, and now it is not only flowing but exploding, like a dragon spewing indiscriminate flame in all directions, beyond any measure of control. I hate everything. I hate me. All the love in my heart is veiled by rage.

Sometime later, as the anger finally subsides, all my wits are exhausted, and I cling to love again, but now it is from a place of shame. Not only have I terrified my children or made a spectacle of myself, but I am also a thirty-nine-year-old, generally kind, professional woman who, it turns out, can't handle her shit. *sigh*

Over time, shame slowly gives way to rest, and if I do not spend some real work on it, the whole cycle starts again next time, despite all the hope for it to be different.

* * *

I am currently reading *My Grandmother's Hands* by Resmaa Menakem, and he describes the states of our lizard brain/vagus nerve as rest, fight, flight, and freeze, which are all familiar. But he also describes the lesser-explored *annihilate* mode, which is when the body reacts with a "last ditch" effort of survival against some threat (real or imagined).

He writes that *fight* is to *annihilate* as *punch* is to *decapitate*.[15]

As I read this, I have an instant recognition: in these extreme moments, where I feel utterly beyond control, I am getting to this *annihilate* place. The question is: *why*? Why do I perceive this situation as deeply threatening?

While I sometimes rise to leadership, I have also always had a feeling of discomfort at being "in charge," where the danger is that I might be revealed as being truly powerless. I see that this feeling was exacerbated by childhood bullying and by messages I inherited. Even with people I loved as a child, I had the common experience that standing out was associated with ridicule or disapproval.

In fact, when I really look at it, this pattern has shaped how I view love itself. Somewhere along the way, I authored a story that to love someone is to relinquish all my power to them. And conversely, to stand in my power with someone means I do not love them. Yikes—thanks for that tricky one, dear subconscious. I love my children perhaps most deeply than all the people in this whole world, certainly the most unconditionally. My whole life has greater meaning because of their existence. Loving them is like breathing air—it is everywhere, in everything, the most natural thing that is impossible to do without. And the depth of love is met with a corresponding pull to give away all my power. A pull that I must fight in order to maintain some sense of authority or even autonomy. Paradoxically, *love* for someone sets me up to open this core wound of powerlessness.

So, here I am, the mom meant to be in control of the situation yet totally powerless to stop the misbehavior. My bias of

---

15 Resmaa Menakem, *My Grandmother's Hands: Racialized Trauma and the Pathway to Mending Our Hearts and Bodies* (Las Vegas: Central Recovery Press, 2017).

powerlessness is confirmed, my very being is under threat of ridicule, rejection, and unacceptability. My dragon roars as I surge into annihilate mode.

* * *

For a long time, I certainly took in messages that anger was real, but it wasn't to be talked about or worked with after the fact. It should be tucked away from view after it passes. I only doubled down on this story as I became a mother. I thought "good" moms didn't get angry. Nobody talked about how it's possible to get so furious, even with an infant, that you have to just leave the room out of fear of your own actions. Each of the countless times that this has happened to me, I feel driven to confront my anger, to really see it, to unhook it from my system. Of course, this comes with strings attached—a barely conscious subtext that utters, "This damn well better work. I better come out of this less angry, because obviously my anger is unacceptable and must, therefore, be dealt with." I've been so active in shunning this side of myself. But what if anger were normalized for us parents? How could we show up, our anger as a voice of necessary boundaries and protection? Could we look at anger with fresh eyes, as something to be curious about rather than hide?

I believe in the idea of using my anger as power for good, even for loving action. I just don't seem to naturally harness anger until the point when it gets absolutely overwhelming. It's all or nothing with me. I want this dragon to remain fierce and powerful but not to take over so all I can see is fiery, blind rage. I want to find the reins of my anger and fly it to something that actually *works* in my life.

A couple of months ago, my daughter splashed water out of the bathtub. She knows this is not allowed, but normally, for something small like this, I might just ignore it or let it slide until the misbehavior was more egregious, potentially without even realizing I was doing so. This time, I had that flash of irritation and took immediate action, reminding her that this was not okay. She took it in stride (instead of starting a whine-fest, which I was worried about) and actually seemed *happier* in the next few minutes. I realized at that moment that she needs extremely well-attended boundaries. If I mark them for her early and often, she relaxes, and *she knows she's safe*. If I miss this early moment, her behavior is much more likely to snowball into the utterly atrocious, because she's looking for the boundary and needs to see me holding the container for her. If I am really attentive and vigilant, I can catch these moments and nip them in the bud. I can use the early kernels of anger to keep my children safe.

So, now I turn to my anger, my dragon. I can perhaps treat this anger like I treat her—watch it like a hawk and, the moment the dragon rears its head even for a peek, see it and channel it into something supportive, like naming a boundary or moving my body in a healing way. My anger needs my attention, not dismissal, fixing, or dismantling. I get to let my dragon live on and flourish, without wasting resources on flame-throwing. Like all the good things, this will require mindfulness, patience, and lots of practice.

SPIT IT OUT

LYNN BROMLEY

In honor and recognition of Ketanji Brown Jackson,
the first Black woman nominated to the Supreme Court of
the United States of America

"Don't swallow," I want to tell her.
"Just spit it out, right there on the floor—that acrid, viscous
mess that was coaxed and
        then required that you take.
That you take like it's just fine.
That you take as if you deserve it."

But she can't spit it out while they watch.
"So don't swallow," I want to tell her.
She must say what they want—it's the password.

And when she has to smile and pretend that she likes it,
I want to yell to her, "Don't swallow!"

The words and acquiescence that betray her to herself,
that she does for all of us.
"Hold it in, sister, 'til we've got you," I want us all to say.

"Don't swallow.
Your head may appear bowed to their insistence,
but we see it where it really is—high
    above the bullies' pleasure, far beyond their imagining.
Spit it out. Spit it out now!"

"We've got you.
We'll wipe your eyes. We'll wipe up the floor.
We'll give you a cool drink, help you fix your lipstick, and
rub your back while you
Spit   It   Up   And   Out
as many times as it takes to
feel clean."

We've got you.

As Ketanji Brown Jackson, the first Black woman nominated to serve on the Supreme Court, entered the Senate Judiciary Committee room for her public hearing on March 21, 2022, we watched. She walked deliberately, leading a cadre of family, friends, and supporters. She smiled genuinely, convincingly, perhaps even joyously, knowing all she had done to get to this place—knowing the enormity of this day for all of us.

Ketanji Brown Jackson was one of the most qualified nominees of the Supreme Court of the United States to appear before the Senate Judiciary Committee, whose job it is to provide "advice and consent" to the full Senate that the nominee is qualified. Some members of the Committee noted the import of the day and the superb qualifications of this nominee. The Republican members did something else. They debased themselves and the institution in an attempt to debase her—not the first woman, but the first Black woman to be so nominated. She was afforded none of the respect, and certainly none of the fawning praise, that was heaped on the previous nominees—white, male, conservative, and unnecessarily self-declared Christians. And worse . . . it seemed her stellar qualifications were irrelevant.

Never mind that she graduated magna cum laude with a bachelor of arts in government from Harvard Radcliffe Institute or that she received a Juris Doctor cum laude from Harvard Law School, where she served as a supervising editor for the famed *Harvard Law Review*.

Never mind that she was no elite legacy student. She went to public school in Miami, Florida, growing up in a very modest home. Her parents studied in segregated schools, attended historically Black colleges, and began their careers as public-school teachers in the Miami-Dade public school system. Her father started law school when Ketanji was in grade school, and she speaks of sitting next to him in their apartment in the evenings. While he tackled his law school homework, she worked on her preschool coloring books.[16] What a great story. What a great example of American opportunity . . . if you're white, that is, and even better if you're a man.

Never mind that she serves as proof of the concept that it's possible for a hard-working, ordinary Black girl from an ordinary public school to study hard and work even harder in order to rise to the greatest court in the land—perhaps better referred to as the "greatest" court in the land.

Never mind that her resume got even more impressive after Harvard as the official opinion of the New York City Bar Association's notes.

---

16 "Ketanji Brown Jackson," Biography, March 7, 2022, https://www. biography.com/law-figure/ketanji-brown-jackson.

For the past 150 years, the New York City Bar Association has been evaluating judicial candidates in a non-partisan manner based on the nominee's competence and merit, rating the nominees as Qualified, Highly Qualified, or Not Qualified. They not only evaluated her as "Highly Qualified" but they also went on to commend her further:

> Judge Jackson's record reflects a very thoughtful, detail-oriented, and temperate jurist free from partiality. Her written opinions are well-organized, thoroughly researched, persuasive, and accessible, embodying judicial clarity and restraint while reflecting her command of a range of subjects and diverse tools of legal reasoning. Judge Jackson's colleagues confirm that she will have a strong ability to build consensus as part of a panel. Her work demonstrates her understanding and appreciation of the role of the judiciary. Widespread praise from Judge Jackson's colleagues on and off the bench, as well as practitioners who appeared before her, focused on Judge Jackson's respectful manner of communicating with others, thorough preparation, exceptional writing skills, ability to synthesize and convey complex legal issues with ease, and ideal judicial temperament. Judges appointed by both parties characterized Judge Jackson as objective, unbiased, fair, and humble, observing that she never appeared to reach conclusions based on a predetermined bias on any issue.[17]

---

17 Judiciary Committee, "Report on the Nomination of the Honorable Ketanji Brown Jackson to the Supreme Court of the United States," New York City Bar, April 1, 2022, https://www.nycbar.org/member-and-career-services/committees/reports-listing/reports/detail/nomination-of-judge-ketanji-brown-jackson.

Never mind that the Committee members could've showcased this lovely and uplifting example of what can happen when opportunity and diligence intersect. Instead, these primarily old, white men looked down from the imposing judicial architecture that places them literally above the nominee and interrogated her on ungermane subjects, interrupted her, and reminded her repeatedly that she would not be afforded the space and grace offered to the male nominees who came before her.

Then they started with their illogical and illegal questions. One senator asked, "Are babies racist?" and another asked Judge Ketanji Brown Jackson, "Can you define 'woman' for me?" And then the illegal question, the one that is an insult to the Constitution—the document based on the separation of church and state—that they and she must swear an oath to defend: "Do you go to church? May I ask what church you go to?"

My anger rises now as I write this in the same way it did when I witnessed it. In the past few decades, I've experienced, written and spoken about, advocated for, and organized against gender injustice many, many, many, many times. My words/these words now are sickeningly similar to those of my past, save for this difference: there isn't the accompanying rage of my past. I instead wonder if the work of my generation and the ones before has made any difference at all. My anger feels less righteous than it feels old and rotten. and rotting. It's black and foul-smelling, and I don't know where to put it. I can't spit it out; I'm full up from swallowing, and I'm worried about spilling it at the feet of our daughters. It wants to burn. I want it to burn away.

Pictures and images of past and present are reeled up in a loop, playing and replaying in my mind. They are triggered by the news of the day, the news of yesterday, and what I expect will be the news of tomorrow. The images are of women and me, and other women and me, and more women and me . . . all doing and saying things we *don't* want to be doing or saying for a calculated greater good, which is simply survival for most of us, perhaps progress for some. The reel is old, but the content is as relevant as it is obscene and perverse . . . and it's achingly exhausting to view and review this content.

Enter Mighty Girl with her flamethrower. She's a brave and steady companion who accompanies me in all the places where power is uneven, where I (and those like me) are not welcomed or where we are simply invisible. I met her in my early days. She would be the one to remind me, after the fact, of what I *should* have said or done instead of receding or remaining silent in tacit agreement.

As my experience and the years went on, Mighty Girl and I worked more seamlessly together. Our after-the-fact conversations began to happen in real time. She would lend me her courage and toss me the words and the attitude so I could land them in the room. These days, she mostly follows me around and hides in the margins, waiting for my call.

Once summoned, Mighty Girl enters the architecture of inquisition, the Senate Judiciary Committee hearing room. She turns up the flame, and all are startled by the sudden *whoosh*. She points it at the offending structures, and wood and rugs and chairs and paper and patriarchy burst into flame. She saves the raised bench of inquisition for last so our mob can gather and cheer as it turns to ashes, rendering the former occupant/senators small and laughable without the trappings of power.

"Are babies racist?" What a stupid question.

What is the definition of a woman? Seriously? Are you seriously asking that?

Do you go to church? Aha! A trick question, as we all know the Constitution makes it illegal to ask that.

I delight in remembering Mighty Girl, but I don't summon her today. Today, my anger is tired. Chronic sexism and injustice have carried me so far past anger that I don't know if I could find my way back. I'm not even certain that I want to.

This place past anger isn't a place I ever wanted to be. I'm embarrassed to be here. Instead, I imagined islands of respite, places to stop a bit to rejoice in a battle won or nearly won, to appreciate one another, and to share our stories of triumph and defeat—those same stories that we would want to pass along to our sisters to come. Together, we would rest and recover until we suit up and resupply for the next fight.

I imagined we could rest on the island of voting rights before the fight for abortion rights; I imagined we could rest on the island of equal access before the fight for marriage equality. I never imagined having to turn back to again win the ground we had gained.

Once again triggered, today's replay is of me four decades past in a job interview. I'm newly graduated, new degree in hand, searching for a teaching job at a time when there was a glut of us. My roommate had taken a job as a "permanent sub," getting a low daily wage but no contract; no benefits; and, of course, no assurance of a job in the next school year. I was interviewing for a teacher's aide position. It was purported to be the way to get into the system. "Do a good job and you might get hired on full time," they said, "or maybe even get your own classroom."

I'm pretty in the way that one is at twenty-two, slender, nice legs, generous and perky breasts. I'm immediately aware of all of these things as I sit across the desk from the principal. He rolls his chair to the side, closer to me but with just enough desk between us to establish who is in charge here.

He asks the usual questions, I assume, yet I only remember two all these years later.

"Are you married?" he asks in a way that I know it's not a yes-or-no question.

"Not yet," I say.

"Are you one of those women's libbers?" he asks me.

I desperately want to say, "Excuse me?" in part to catch my breath as I think of an answer but mostly to signal my opinion of the question. I dare not, so I do not. I need the job.

"Not really," I say. I know he's thinking of bra-burning, hairy-legged "feminists," and I want to say I'm not like "those women," even though I am so much more like them than the woman he's trying to hire.

That isn't enough for him. He pauses for a long time, so it's up to me to say the next thing. I say, "Well I certainly believe in equality, but I know I can be the teacher I want to be by day and be home in time to make my husband's dinner." I didn't have a husband. I don't know why I didn't say "family." It was all I could choke out.

I didn't get the job. It was a teacher's aide job, when I was fully trained and certified to be a teacher. I didn't know then to be angry. Instead, I felt shame—shame that I couldn't find a job with my bachelor's degree in English and my minor in education, my 3.6 GPA, and my certificate that said I was qualified and had completed the necessary student teaching. With that and more that I so wanted to bring, still I couldn't get a job as a teacher's aide. I didn't get the job because I didn't hide my women's libber tendencies well enough. *Why didn't I just say "no" instead of "not really,"* I asked myself.

Mighty Girl was in her infancy then, and without her full complement of tools and attitude, she could make me feel disquieted by my shame but not fierce like she would in later years. I like what anger and rage can fuel and do. I like how righteous it can feel and how cleansing it can be for a moment. But this place, this place of Tired Anger, has no apparent benefit. My Tired Anger does not resolve . . . I can't even find words to make a summary in order to put a period at the end of any sentence about it . . .

I've fought mightily for decades—marching and protesting, advocating and summoning, writing and speaking out and up. I've worked on campaigns. I've been elected to office and served in the administration of the first Black president. I've worked nearly constantly. I've overachieved and under-enjoyed most of my life for what now seem like very modest gains that are eroding and will need to be regained by a generation we didn't fully prepare.

When I was disquieted, but before I was fierce, I didn't know how to cleverly and demurely and powerfully and strategically answer absurd questions from similarly absurd men. I didn't know how to let them, or even encourage them, to preen while I choked down their scum. I didn't know how to play a seeming sycophant to their unjust power while it was my real power that was on full display for my sisters to witness. I didn't know then how to do what our sister Ketanji Brown Jackson did when she so deftly feigned subservience to answer illogical, illegal, and demeaning questions. In the early years, we hadn't ever seen the likes of it. Mighty Girl and I had to make it up on our own. But now we have. Now our daughters have.

But there's no rejoicing here. I'm angry about that but have insufficient energy to light the flame thrower. My Tired

Anger wants to close its eyes. My Tired Anger wants to set down the flame thrower, but I dare not leave it lying about without the directions. "Prolonged use may result in terminal fatigue."

Know this, my sisters. We're not allowed anger in public. It invalidates the password to the places of power where we are not welcomed but must be.

I weep as I tell you.

We must hold it in.

But we don't have to swallow.

It's with our sisters, with one another, that we can spit it out . . . that we must spit it out.

MARCH MADNESS

∧∧∧∧∧∧∧∧∧

MADELINE MCCLURE

MARCH 2

'M TO WRITE ABOUT ANGER, AN EMOTION I DON'T FEEL.
I could more easily write about the ones that I roll around
in on the daily. Sadness, for example, is easier to manhandle.
It's like sitting in a warm kiddie pool on a cold day, half your
body softening underwater, the other shivering and unsatis-
fied. Or the constant, general feeling of submissive existen-
tialism, from which comes humor and, ultimately, joy. But
anger isn't really on the menu. I've got an intolerance to it.

God, I remember when my first boyfriend told me he'd
been sleeping with my close friend—the beautiful, blonde
Tara—for six months, how my mind went fathomlessly blank,
only a relentless tinnitus in its place. I recall I said the word
"what?" over and over, feeling as if my head were an old steel
bell struck by some god in the sky. The unbelievable had happened, and I could only express profound surprise.

My family had some anger, though I think back on it lov-
ingly. My older sister Clio was so easy to make mad. All I had
to do was impose a little and she would throw a shoe at me.
My mom tells a story about driving us one day in rural Vir-
ginia in the late eighties, yelling about something. I leaned

over and started pinching her upper arm like a little tickle. "What are you doing?" she asked, trying to keep her eyes on the road.

"Theeeere's a witch in theere!" I sang to her with glee.

* * *

MARCH 5

I do feel generationally angry, in a Simpsons kind of way. Every generation has gotten angrier since *The Simpsons*, the birthplace of cartoon's cynical parodies. Homer became Cartman and then Peter, which is now apparently *American Dad*. What was life like before *The Simpsons*? We'll never know.

* * *

MARCH 6

If anger did live in me, it would be nestled deep within the soft walls of my throat. Not a place where my voice emerges from but somewhere that smoke could reach as if to blanket, somewhere that the voice passes over. I think about how I reach for a cigarette when I feel perturbed. But then, I'm calm and collected, soothed by the inhaling pucker, the two involved fingers and flicking thumb. Usually, I continue to feel pissed when the depleted cigarette is snubbed out, but now it's been tucked to bed in the back there, like a little lump.

Once, I was sober and smoke-free for a long time, about six months, and I started to dance with a group of hippies to EDM and "international" music. I felt really angry at myself when I danced and angry at everyone. I felt really angry all of the time, actually. It was as if there weren't any protection between the space inside my chest and the rest of the world. It felt fiery and manic, and when I danced, I cried hot, fucked-up tears.

* * *

MARCH 8

When I was a kid, my mom always tried to call me Mad. "Who's Mad?!" I'd announce, "I'm not Mad!"

* * *

MARCH 10

The other nickname I did not take strongly to was "the picker." Childhood photos show me riddled in neon Band-Aids from some scrape or bite that had repeatedly been peeled raw. A small indentation took residence on the ball of my right foot thanks to nightly needling of this spot. There was no logical reason for this, only that it felt as if something were buried there that needed to be removed. I was a joyful child, covered in scabs.

* * *

MARCH 11

My high school history teacher, Ms. McMather, wore different colored socks under her crocks and sweater vests and displayed her brittle hair in a chaotic halo. She had eyes like a hawk, beady and searching. She seemed to spot every offense that happened in her room and also seemed to take joy in mocking these offenses, no matter how small. "Wesley, stop acting like a monkey," she might say to the budding queer boy. "Use your head for once," she'd announce to the class. I considered her to be incredibly lonely in a small house, perhaps without electricity. Her anger, I imagined, was molded by years of teaching public school in a small, rainy town. And it scared me. I would tease her with my friends, her witch-like demeanor.

Years later, I ran into her when I was checking out at the food co-op. *"Madeline McClure?"* I heard in an astonished but joyful tone. I turned and nearly dropped my avocado.

"McMather!" I yelped to a retired Ms. McMather and looked at her in surprise and slight terror, then relief, and then guilt. We caught up briefly. Her loneliness returned to me, and this time, I saw myself in it.

* * *

MARCH 13

I'm not really angry at anything, I think and root around my body with the teeth of some tweezers for an evening.

* * *

MARCH 14

What cultural references do we have for anger? For (white) women, there's the archetypal witch and the looney housewife banging a cast iron pan over her husband's head. I heeded a "don't get mad, get even" philosophy from a young age, choosing to pull elaborate pranks or simply annoy the shit out of my opponents. I've looked into the origins of this phrase and was surprised to find that it's attributed to John F. Kennedy's description of Boston politics. To think, all this time I've been following in the masculine American tradition of civic retribution. And I could've been a witch.

* * *

MARCH 15

I aspire to Patti Smith anger, but I think I come off more as a quietly fuming *Pleasantville*.

* * *

MARCH 16

I chart my anger in the moments that light a cigarette in my chest. Some are obvious: Charley interrupting me after talking for forty minutes without pause, his dry voice booming in an effort to overcome my own. The wealthy and, generally, this fucking country. A thinly veiled insult directed straight toward me. Others surprise me: An attractive gap in a girl's teeth after my parents put braces on mine. My dog insistently licking her paw. Angry at myself for buying weed at a slick store and for running out of weed. The memory of a distant ex laughing too loudly at me and how I felt burning humiliation. Humiliation as a reaction in place of anger. Why am I angry only at myself in the moment and angry at others in memory?

* * *

MARCH 21

I'm five years older than the internet, which is to say that it's in the early-thirties phase of starting to think about therapy. The internet has fiery, chaotic anger, from incel and white supremacist manifestos to the Facebook face-offs that have forever mutated the holidays. Us early internet foragers stumble around the net like children having a temper tantrum in the cereal aisle.

In another twenty years, maybe the internet will have a more nuanced anger. I imagine a landscape of mature rage, fully realized through emojis. For instance, we need acronyms for anger in the same way we have them for joy. What will be the angry equivalent of LOL and LFG? I propose screaming out loud, SOL, and LNFG, let's not fucking go.

* * *

MARCH 22

I'm not an angry person, but in fourth grade, I was suspended for kneeing Sam Crawley in the balls. I most vividly remember his face, how red it became, and later, my father's face, crimson with rage.

* * *

MARCH 28

There's a reel on social media of a white woman drawly explaining an aspect of white supremacy: White women don't have internal power in society. White women find security and power through the white men in our lives, through sexual exploitation of our bodies and emotional manipulation, principally through victimization. The angry Black woman trope is potent in this landscape—powerful, embodied anger is delegitimized. This reel has my head throbbing. Anger is not a privilege, but it's not a tool that I inherited. I inherited being the entertainer, and when that doesn't fit the bill, I can cry big, fat tears.

* * *

MARCH 31

Will I ever truly be angry? Am I angry all of the time? Humor and shame, sadness, loneliness—these would be so much easier to write about. I'm sitting in a pool; it's lukewarm, and I'm never satisfied.

When my mom was angry with my sister and I, she would say we were in "hot water." I love her for this. It was scary to be in her hot water, and it put us in line. When my dad was angry, he would storm out. Now, I'm an adult, and though I'm surrounded by storms growing ever more violent, the water is gentle. Feel my hands; they've softened so much that they barely feel a thing.

WHAT'S THE WORST THAT CAN HAPPEN?

∧∧∧∧∧∧∧∧∧∧∧∧∧∧

MARY ANKER

A NGER AND I SHARE A LIFE. SHE THINKS OF ME AS A VESSEL. Pours herself in like molten gold. I think of her as a sparkling supplement. Giving me energy, a way to cope, and lots of verve. Anger's heat can overwhelm, often suddenly. She can be a troublemaker as well as a protector. We have rough times. Go on wild joy rides. Disappoint each other. Our volatility is exhausting, but we keep the passion. Navigating the reckless and wondrous for seventy-five years.

I remember:

1947, when I was told "Hush" and railed against that dismissal. Anger and I cried into eventual submission. I played in the red dirt and picked desert sand from eyes, nose, and ears. Chased tumble weeds in the heat of Las Cruces, New Mexico. My first home, adobe with dirt floors. One day, a neighborhood mother pierced the ears of all the one-year-old girls. Imagine my mother returning home from work–there I was with slim gold rings in my tiny lobes.

The '50s. In Long Beach, California, parents used the free-rein, free-range method to raise children. Kids roamed without supervision. Settled our own fights. Ate lunch at the nearest house but were in trouble if we weren't home by 4:00 p.m. For every minute past four, a switch on my bare legs. Belts, brooms, wooden spoons, all means of teaching a lesson, accompanied by, "This hurts me more than it does you." Anger and I rejected unfairness. Stood up for my sister and brothers. Nursed hurt feelings by enjoying tantrums. Sent to my room to "Tame your Irish temper." Once there, Anger fueled me as we threw clothes out of drawers, and then, as tears dried, she simmered on low as I re-folded and organized neat, calming piles. Sitting still on a stool, watching a clock . . . another way to tame us. Punishments turned the burning in me into a serene strength.

Anger taught me not to cower no matter what. Refusing to do boring workbooks or come in after recess at the public school, I found my ruffian self at St. Joseph's. There, we prayed. There, kids were hit and humiliated. I read the lives of saints. Once, I pressed a rose thorn into my scalp, copying St. Teresa to suffer for my sins. I loved my teacher, Sister Cora, who had a class of sixty and was also the principal. The consequences for my bad conduct ran from dusting and vacuuming the convent to standing in the back of the classroom with my nose touching the wall. Anger hated that one. ADHD wasn't known yet, and Sister Cora, in her kind wisdom, did her best. She didn't hit. I graduated with a love of writing. Prayers became a mantra.

In 1960, my parents' marriage was rocky. My mother told my dad, "Either we all move somewhere together and start over or you move out." We moved to a four-room house on a cattle ranch in the foothills of the Sierra Nevadas. A real little surfer girl from Long Beach, I tried my best to fit into the horse-and-gun culture.[18] My dad taught us how to shoot a rifle. We bought a horse named Tex and two German shepherds. I shared a bedroom with my two younger brothers; a kitchen, closet, and bathroom with the whole family. My parents slept in the other room next to my mom's baby grand piano. I missed my brilliant sister, who had left for college. A lot of change and rupture. It was hard to adapt, to find friends. Kids were tough.

Lonely and alone, Anger and I cried when we rode Tex after school. The smell of dry, evergreen chaparral and the soft snorts from Tex soothed us. As a freshman, I was suspended from Mariposa County High School for fighting. Down and dirty fighting. Her fist from behind. Nails deep in my face. Anger and I thrilled to slug this girl back. She represented all that was wrong. My mother called me an embarrassment. As I tried to be a good 4-H member, I also had no qualms about lying so I could be with a boy my dad described as "too old."[19] Things were falling apart.

Word must have gone out to the family that I needed help. My sister now lived with her husband and baby. Taking the bus alone from Merced to visit them in Berkeley, I felt cool and independent. Everything about their lives was foreign. I barely understood them, their friends, the vocabulary, that confidence. I realized that smart people were cool, and humor could be sophisticated; I felt sad and left out. On the long ride home, Anger came to me as revelation. I made a palpable turning of direction.

---

18 Beach Boys. "Surfer Girl." Track 1 on *Surfer Girl*. Capital Records. 1963.

19 "4-H Homepage," 4-H, accessed July 13, 2022, https://4-h.org/.

I started to study. Hard. I paid attention as if my life depended on it. After two years in the mountains, we sold our horse, gave our dogs to friends, and moved to the San Joaquin Valley. Another new culture. My dad bought an O'Day Day Sailer, and we found peace and fun on Lake Millerton. My high school guidance counselor dismissed the idea that I could make California Scholarship Federation lifetime membership.[20] Anger wanted to slap her. I wanted to cry, but instead, we graduated with that golden rope over my robe and a tiny pin that I still have. And with that honor came scholarships.

I landed in Oregon, back with nuns. Again, praying and peace. A future in mind. When I came home for the summer and told my dad I was going to work in Tahoe, he said, "No, you're not." No discussion. Anger helped channel my seething. I became a reporter and photographer for the *Madera Daily Tribune*, had a two-way radio installed in our family car, and covered the police beat, taking pictures of car wrecks, observing crime scenes, and visiting the jail and the sheriff on my rounds. Toward the end of a record hot summer, my editor gave me the assignment of a lifetime. I interviewed as many people over ninety as I could find for the County Fair Edition.

Those interviews took place on old porches. Listening to the stories of lives that started around 1876—the wars, the inventions, the struggles, loves, and losses—and then, the advice offered. I wrote of these incredible survivors with a yearning and a love for them and the insights of their long view. Their faces and voices were witnesses to an understanding that only comes with time and reckoning with oneself.

---

20 "CSF Membership," CSF, accessed July 13, 2022, https://csf-cjsf.org/membership/.

Everything about them was now at an accepting ease. The dry heat of the Central Valley turned my face deep red, and one old-timer said to me, chuckling, "Don't think about the heat, then it can't get to you." Anger was nowhere to be found.

In 1968, I graduated from my women's college. I had been the editor of our newspaper, *The Mirror,* and wrote about prayer versus LSD and about living a beautiful, quiet life along the Willamette River juxtaposed with the controversial war in Vietnam. As freshmen in 1964, we were encouraged to be "lovely ladies," and by our junior year, Betty Friedan and Bella Abzug were showing us how to be women warriors. I was elected to Who's Who among American Universities and Colleges, but no matter.[21] Not all change was fast. Free love was easy. Employment was not.

My first jobs were in advertising, working for men who called me "their girl." First, I was a receptionist and wrote ads from home. Next, I was a copywriter who was paid overtime. After a positive interview at *The Oregonian,* I was told they had hired a young man, my competition, as a reporter because I was "just going to get married anyway." I was a frustrated and furious English major/journalism minor with reporting experience. To help with rent and expenses, I cleaned my landlord's house and babysat his five children. Anger came bounding back.

During a march for civil rights, men spat at us. When marching against the war in Vietnam, we were called dirty commies. As upset as I had been when President Kennedy, Martin Luther King Jr., Bobby Kennedy, Malcolm X, and Kent

---

21 "Who's Who Among American High School Students," Wikipedia, last modified January 22, 2022, https://en.wikipedia.org/wiki/Who%27s_Who_Among_American_High_School_Students.

State students were shot, somehow I was still proud, if somewhat shell-shocked, to be an American. Television brought this war right to us, and what we saw and heard wreaked chaos within us. Anger and I protested. Injustice was everywhere. My dad, a Purple Heart Iwo Jima Marine, didn't stop me when I said I was leaving the United States. My mother worried about me going alone.

I left the country with my pitiful savings and a one-way ticket. Determination to find some purpose aligned itself with dismay at the violent reactions to war protests, the civil rights movement, and the women's movement. Anger felt a lot like fear as we landed in Paris. At a Mao rally, we were surprised to learn the French despised Americans. I was naïve, stupid, and low on funds. My idea of becoming an expatriate writer was just that, an idea. Not a plan. Anger turned on me. *What could you have been thinking?* she asked again and again. I became wily. I became "from Canada" and applied for jobs listed in the *Herald Tribune*. Despair took Anger's place.

I wrote my way into a job as a nanny for an American family in Moscow, USSR. I don't remember how I told my parents. There were only expensive payphones, and my French . . . too poor to make a collect call. I hitchhiked my way to Germany where a friend lived so I could pass US clearance and make reservations on the weekly train from Paris to Moscow. I was down to ten dollars. I left my battered copy of *Europe on 5 Dollars a Day* behind.

It was the eve of 1970. Traveling from Hamburg, we crossed through West Berlin, past the wall into East Berlin, on and on to Warsaw, and then into *Doctor Zhivago* country. Days of snow for miles. A few tiny, brown villages. In Minsk, the train's wheels were adjusted to accommodate the smaller USSR tracks. I arrived on Christmas day with one backpack and nothing warm enough for Moscow's winter. No one to meet me. The Russian language gives away no clues. The alphabet is code. No smiles to be seen or returned. I was numb physically and emotionally but warming with a sense of daring after arriving, literally, in enemy territory.

It was the Cold War. Other American nannies and I talked about being free while all around us were not. As Americans, we felt safe in this dangerous place. We weren't supposed to, but we made friends with Soviets. I took care of three children and all the housekeeping. On our one day and night off, we went out. A guard was stationed outside our apartment complex. We were followed. Getting on a bus meant people hitting each other's backs to jam on as many as possible. The inside windows were frosted in thick ice. We met Europeans and Soviets at the dollar bars. My friend Victoria, who had been a volunteer in Vietnam, and I started a catering business for embassy people. We hitched rides home on military trucks, the only option late at night. When the soldiers found out that we were *Amerikansky*, they were happily astonished. They knew some English. We knew a bit of Russian. They dropped us a few blocks from our building so our guard wouldn't see them. We were also friends with US Marines who guarded the embassy and the Navy Seals who were there to do something secret.

It was surreal: Old women, *babushkas*, shoveling the sidewalks and streets. Everyone drinking lots of vodka to stay warm inside and out. My boss, wandering the streets of Moscow in the middle of the night with cameras hanging under his coat. During my own late nights, I watched huge missiles or bombs being transported. I witnessed people freezing to death, slumped against gray buildings. Being an American was a lucky accident of birth. I became a patriot. People who live under oppression are not dirty, but the people in their governments are. I thought I was worldly. I thought I was growing up.

I was in big trouble. Frozen. Pregnant. Panicked. Anger, despair, fear, guilt—all were with me. After no help at the US embassy, I went to a Soviet clinic where the doctor said, "*Bolshoi.*" She arranged for an abortion. I told my American family I was staying with friends for a long weekend. The procedure took place without anesthesia. Complications kept me in the hospital no matter how I tried to convince them I was okay. When I didn't come home on time, the family was rightfully worried, and the embassy put out an alert. I had a lot of questions to answer during intense interrogations. All with Americans. All with men. Between caring for the children and awkward silences with my bosses, I questioned myself. No easy answers. After leaving Moscow, I wandered around Europe with a friend and tried to heal.

The '70s and '80s sped up. I finally made it home. Older, maybe wiser, I was determined to, as my dad used to say, "Straighten up and fly right." The term "self-care" wasn't a thing in the '70s. In a world led by Gloria Steinem and *Ms.* magazine, we were redefining what it meant to be a woman, to establish a career, to find ourselves, to vote for our rights. I landed a teaching job, got married, and mistakenly thought I was well on my way. That marriage was annulled quickly. I quit the teaching position I loved. We were the children of the Greatest Generation, and I wasn't feeling great. I ignored Anger when she showed up. I thought about moving to Hawaii. She was furious at me as I realized we weren't going anywhere . . . again. She was incredulous.

Something was different this time. I had been nowhere before. I righted myself. The familiarity of no plan was now a no-panic comfort, a strength. The irony of this pattern, a path. First, get a job. Second, find your own place to live. Stay calm. Set achievable goals. Anchor with your friends. The constant emotional roller coaster of my life was slowing down on a level track. I had a challenging job with responsibility, even a title. I was finishing my master's degree. I felt secure. Secure enough to love wholeheartedly, to marry Art Anker, and to have children. We took a leap and moved from Oregon to New York.

I should have known that wherever you go, there you are. It took being a mother to finally acknowledge that Anger and I had a problem. In a flash of impatience, I raised my hand to hit my daughter. I did not hit her, but Anger leaked out all the time. The day before my first therapy appointment, I threw a tuna sandwich across the room and went upstairs, cringing. My four-year-old was cleaning the wall when I came back. I felt low. On edge. I needed help.

My first therapist was a Jungian psychiatrist. We went deep and dark and sad. It was an intellectual and emotional stretch. Intimidating. I worked to understand archetypes, the unconscious, and complexes. I looked at my various selves and anger's role in my personal history. How it could hurt and help me. I began to accept anger as a natural emotion, not as an inevitable character flaw. I thought my doctor was helping me control my reactions. I misunderstood that control was not the goal. I thought my inside feelings and my outward response to them came as one. It felt that way. It looked that way. Something was still missing.

The '90s and 2000s saw a lot more moves. A lot more life. More therapists. Three daughters making their way. Our family handling the fear around Art's heart attack and stroke and my breast cancer. Art's international traveling taking him away even more. All of us worrying about him. The peak of my teaching career and the beginning of poetry. Finally, both of us exiting the workforce. I was surprised that I continued to feel anger, less often though. I thought that with less pressure and more time, I'd have more control. Still, that control issue. Still, that missing something. Anger hounds me. Confounds me still.

It's my second daughter, a life coach, who's teaching me, at seventy-five, that all emotions are allowed to be felt. Repeat. Anger is an allowed feeling. Invite it in. Abby gently reminds me, "All feelings are okay; all behaviors are not." I had named it, blamed it, and felt ashamed. My behavior was my reaction to this human emotion. I did everything but let myself feel hurt, fear, shock, frustration, and sadness. Abby says there's no controlling anger or any other emotion. There's only letting yourself feel. Sounds simple.

It isn't. The hard part is practicing patience. To consciously decide. To physically feel. To let the emotion be on me—not become me. To fume and cry. To feel out of control—not act out of control. The easy part comes with the relief of feeling the emotion slip away. You can't have one without the other. Don't rush. Once I let myself recognize the heat of anger and sit with it, I begin to feel a cooling calm. I feel angry. I'm not anger. It's at this point that I understand who's knocking at the door. As the emotion is disarmed, empathy and perception gradually arrive. That old, bad conduct of yelling, slamming, flouncing. . . transforms into let's put this out on the table and take a look.

"Allow yourself to feel it, Mom. What's the worst that can happen?"

It turns out that the worst never happens. People don't stop loving me. No silent treatment. My inner and outer selves merge. Compatibly. With recognition, the dark dissipates into the mirror. Anger is an emotion, not a person. I feel it; then I meet myself with ease, honesty, and kindness. We're older now. We accept each other for what we are. What we're becoming. A soft-strong woman with strong-felt emotions.

THE SECRET

MARY CLARE WOJCIK

I HAVE A SECRET. IT HAS BEEN WITH ME FROM THE TIME I WAS little. This secret was so hush-hush that my body even hid it from me. My body had encapsulated it to keep me safe. My conscious mind may have forgotten, but my body remembered.

As such secrets go, there were clues . . . memories of the smell of the house, adults whispering behind closed doors that night, and flashes of a picture of Jesus hanging on the wall.

I was so little when the event happened that I thought I made it up. The truth is, I questioned more than just the memory of it. Did it really happen? Could I trust myself? Beyond the questioning, I had this nagging feeling of isolation. There was anger and reactivity that I couldn't explain or shake. I didn't know where it was coming from, but the emotion itself was a sign that my survival mechanisms were kicking in.

I understand now that I had become a third party in my own life that night. When I look at pictures of myself from grade school, I can see I was a shell. My eyes looked empty. My spirit stood outside my body, somehow separate, an outsider. As it so often goes with unhealed trauma, I felt shattered into pieces, scared and alone. No one saw the true me; they just saw my shadow, and so did I. I was so disconnected from my true self because of the trauma that my survival mechanisms were in overdrive, and everyone I saw felt like the enemy. I had become a magnet for chaos and easy prey for mean girls; anger was my fortress.

I carried such heavy emotions for a little girl. I knew something was wrong, but I didn't know why. I had experienced a major traumatic event, and yet, no one ever mentioned it afterwards. I had walked through life feeling broken, not realizing I had PTSD. Could I have lived a more peaceful and happy life if someone had talked to me about what had happened? Why had no one told me? Why had they let me struggle? Who were they to take my peace from me?

I remember walking home from school one day, and my friend Laura saying to me, "you are never happy." She was right. I had happy moments for sure, but happy was not my state of being. I was on the defensive most of the time, protecting myself against anything that might cause me harm. I didn't need armor; my anger and reactivity did that for me. I locked myself away, keeping the outside world out.

As I grew, my feeling of brokenness gave rise to a deep depression that I had a hard time digging out of as a teenager. Everything felt heavy, and I had a hard time coping with life—my dad's failing health, a rocky relationship with my mom, and high school drama—and there was also more abuse. Was the word "victim" written on my forehead?

I tried to release my anger and heaviness by purging food, but that just pushed my anger deeper. I tried to gain control of my life by controlling my weight, which landed me in the hospital with a full-fledged eating disorder diagnosis.

Counseling helped with food, but it didn't get to the root cause. So, I numbed myself with exercise and shopping, living out the belief that I was unworthy.

In my early twenties, a doctor explained to me that only a small percentage of people with eating disorders actually get well. I made a decision then and there that I would be in the minority. Through doing inner work, an outpatient program, and support from my compassionate family and friends, I beat it. I beat the eating disorder, but I was still depressed, I was still angry and reactive. There was so much that pointed to the fact (from my perspective and belief system) that, underneath it all, I was just plain broken. I accepted it and went on with my life.

I met and married my husband in my thirties, and we started our family. It wasn't until then that I really started to question if there was more to life. And if there was, how could I help my kids find it? As if some higher power heard my question, answers started to appear. In 2001, I was weeks away from giving birth to my second child when I had a prophetic dream about a tragic world event that came true six months later.

What I now refer to as my 9/11 dream, as well as personal events that followed, were a powerful sign that there really was more to life than what I was experiencing. For the first time, I started to take this seriously: pain and suffering are not our true essence. Underneath all the anger, the depression, and feeling victimized, there is light. We can have peace. We can be peace.

In the book I coauthored with Susan Anthony, *Awakened Faith, Learning to Live the Lord's Prayer*, I wrote about how the questions themselves started a chain of incredible events that helped me find my way back to myself.

It was as if, upon hearing my request, God, Source, Love, the Universe—whatever you choose to call our Creator—took a fine-tooth instrument and gently and carefully extracted the shadow from me. I began to understand that peace is the true goal and light my true essence. I had found a path out.

Underneath it all, I found me. Spirituality helped me embrace my gifts and know my true worth. I learned to love myself and know that I am lovable. Still, there was this nagging ache. This unsettled loneliness. These underlying flares of anger. I couldn't quite figure out why I didn't completely feel whole.

It wasn't until twenty-some years into my spiritual journey that my secret came back to light. The memory of the picture of Jesus on the wall showed back up as I was working with an EFT tapping practitioner. (EFT stands for Emotional Freedom Techniques, which is a form of energy psychology). I mentioned to my tapping practitioner that I didn't know if the story was real or not. She offered that we could work on it and see what we could learn. It didn't take long to realize that the story was indeed a real memory from my childhood; I hadn't just made it up.

Bit by bit, the story emerged. The events became clear, and emotions flooded my awareness. I could remember my parents being called. I could remember them picking me up. And I remember them talking about me as if I wasn't there. This secret wound came back detail after detail and, as they hit the surface, brought with it so much anger; it whistled from my veins, steaming as it hit the cool, spring air.

Deep within my soul, I sobbed and moaned as anger and sorrow left my body. As it surfaced, EFT was the eraser that helped me remove the emotion of this event from my neural pathways. I worked to heal it all, and I can now actually look at the event without emotional pain. The suffering around that event was over. The nagging anger, gone.

Each tap whispered to my soul. No wonder . . . No wonder I had no peace. No wonder I directed anger at those who tried to get close. No wonder I had picked myself apart. I didn't invite the abuse; I was just a little girl being herself. I had been treated like an object, and that scar had not been healed.

This event had left my body feeling like scorched earth—charred, immovable, walling off my heart. Other emotions, even positive ones, puddled on the surface of my being or ran off, unfelt. I couldn't take them in. And the anger was a reemerging visitor lashing out as a reminder of my buried secret.

As I reflected on these revelations from my childhood, I didn't want to tell anyone. I didn't want anyone trying to tell me I had made it up. I didn't want to hurt anyone else who was somehow involved. Could I forgive and let it go?

I could now see that all that pent-up anger, frustration, and sorrow had a purpose. It was a mirror to help me find my way through the shadow. It was the trauma peeking out to show me that something still needed healing.

Every emotion has a purpose, and that anger kept rearing its head until it was healed. It was there to remind me that a piece of me was still wounded. It was there to tell me that that part of my past would continue to be part of my present until it was healed. The yearning for peace would continue to be a yearning until I released the anger, removed the shadow on my heart, and nurtured little me.

I'm grateful for the anger. Not only did it signal that something within me needed healing but it also took what was solid and immovable and softened it until it was crumbled ground. It aerated the soil, preparing it for new shoots of life. The veil and its heavy emotions were lifted. I became fused once again to my soul.

I can now be in the present moment without my mind needing to check out. My heart is now open. Like a lotus, it has flowered in the crumbled, softened mud, petals open, a delicate being greeting the sun. There's no reason to hide any longer. I'm safe. I'm in control. I decide who touches me.

I sat on the edge of my stillness, reflecting on the story so many of us share. So many other women who have endured the pain, the humiliation, the shame of being treated like an object. Like me, they find themselves in survival mode. Confused, lost, depressed . . . angry and struggling to remember who they are. I can see the immensity of the problem.

Dear reader, if you are someone who has suffered from abuse, know that you can recover. As Anne Lamott, American novelist and nonfiction writer says, "Whole parts of the world don't think women are people."[22] We have been excluded from the human story, though we are an intricate part of its creation. We have been made to feel less than and told our voices don't matter. But we do matter. You can heal. There are qualified professionals who can help you get to the other side.

That beautiful being that is you . . . remember her? She's still inside of you. Let's go get her. It's time.

---

22 Anne Lamott, "There are no words . . .," Facebook, May 25, 2022, https://z-p3-upload.facebook.com/AnneLamott/posts/556364802518697.

A WOMAN BY ANY OTHER NAME

MEL HILARIO

THE **W**IFE GOT HER MFA IN ENGLISH AND CREATIVE WRIT-ing. It feels like it was so many years ago, and in the time between then and now, she has mostly been trying to live. Her work has appeared on Facebook, Instagram, and an old blog that she can't even access anymore because she hasn't posted in five years—and in internet time that means you're dead, so WordPress deactivated her login. A long time ago, she actually got it together to write a short piece on Spam (the food, not junk email), which appeared in *Reader's Digest* in Asia, and a poem about her dogs in *The Bark* before it got published on glossy paper. She's been a great live-in editor for her spouse, who is also a writer and has a long list of credits. She realizes that it would be helpful if she had a lot of money and/or a wife just like herself. Yes, she is well aware that being the supportive wife is a thing, just like Stephen King and all these other men that have wives "who are also writers" and might also be famous or known, but usually it's the man that everyone knows. The Wife is probably making sure there's bread and milk and coffee, that the cats/dogs/

kids have been fed, that the electric and cable bills have been paid, that we take the car in soon because that gauge light's been on for a few weeks, and somehow she also knows where your belt/phone/keys are. She wiped down the sink, vacuumed, made sure we didn't run out of toilet paper. When you were doubting yourself, she reassured you. When you said, "It's been such a long time for my career to really take off," you said, "You finished a novel and got it published. Many people don't even do that."

She also thought, *Shut the fuck up, you tone-deaf, entitled asshole*, even though she knows he loves and supports her, even though his acknowledgment of her in his last book made her teary. She can't/is afraid to articulate how she's fighting to stay her own person as the world reminds her that her youth and strength and all the glittering potential that goes with them are fading. He will be distinguished, and his curriculum vitae will need editing, and even though you sincerely mean it, you will practice saying, "That's great honey."

* * *

The first time I hit something, really struck something, I was already well-versed in keeping my anger at bay; truthfully, I was stifling it, shoving it back into every cell of my body. In reality, I wanted to bask in my anger like a steamy bath. I wanted to let it glow and grow like a fire.

The Muay Thai conditioning class was only for exercise, something I agreed to at the behest of a friend—not even a friend, but a good acquaintance—because I'd had it with adulting, despite having only been at it for a few years. But a cubicle doesn't take long to drain one's soul from the body, and I thought a pair of gloves might fight off the corporate tapeworm long enough for me to figure out a plan B for my life. I, in effect, would deal with my own conflict by embracing an activity built for conflict.

Boxing gyms (or any place like them) smell . . . unpleasant at best. They're noisy, a flurry of grunts and the timer and the smacking of pads. Cheetah Muay Thai Academy was this plus a tendril of Tiger Balm, filled with mostly men kicking and punching, circling each other like large cats in pursuit. I felt small in their midst, but I wasn't afraid. There was a very real part of my brain that saw fists flying into a bag and thought, *I would like to do that, too.*

* * *

My best friend and I were talking about that part in the movie *Girlfight* when Michelle Rodriguez's character cracks her abusive dad right in the jaw, knocking him off balance.

"This part always makes me think of you," she said.

"Aww. Thanks, girl," I replied, thinking there probably weren't many people who would receive that as sweet, a compliment.

I never had a chance to raise my voice to my father, much less my fist; it was my brother who exchanged blows with him in the kitchen one day. He was sixteen. He got a *good* shot in, and there was a moment when our father paused, almost out of respect and the realization that he could no longer overpower his son the way he was used to doing.

What if *I* had hit my father? Would he have stopped and seen me as a young adult so fed up and frustrated that she was moved to physical action? I had already challenged him verbally—not yelled but simply questioned him, "why? why not?"—literally a word or two. He had devil-glared, screamed "how dare you talk back to me," disgusted at me. (Luckily, I had found it mostly confusing: *this counts as backtalk, really?* I'd thought.) What if I, his daughter, had punched him? Would he have hit me back, thrown me across the room? He allowed my brother his full, blown-out rage; I couldn't even have my words, a flutter of dissent.

* * *

I come from many backgrounds where one is praised for suffering: immigrants, Catholics, military. What a horrible trifecta.

My father was in the Navy. He joined when he was sixteen, traveled, was harassed for being Filipino, and made a life on the pay and benefits. Other than survival—which is no small feat—I don't know that serving in the military served him that well. Follow orders and don't question authority, these were concepts he took right into parenting. I still set clocks to 24:00 format when available. I hate being late. I fear making mistakes.

My mother is a devout Catholic. She had an altar with a cover she crocheted herself, set up with candles, statues, and pictures. A rosary was on the rearview mirror of every car, and she made the sign of the cross after starting the engine. (For a while as an adult, I did this too, thinking, *Well, it can't hurt*.) Once when my brother and I were disobedient and one of us fell, she sat in her schadenfreude and said, "Oh, see! God is punishing you." Follow rules, don't question authority, and you'll be rewarded and loved only if you're obedient, these were concepts she took right into parenting. I often want to please people for all the wrong reasons. I don't often think about pleasing myself.

My parents were immigrants. They both came to the United States as agents of their new country—my father, a sailor; my mother, the daughter of a soldier. Or her father might have been an officer . . . I learned later that he was sort of a secret operative working undercover as a driver for a high-ranking general; that he spoke five languages; and that he had two other families, one in the Philippines and another in Japan.

My maternal grandmother married at the age of nineteen. She was ten years my grandfather's junior, the middle of three daughters in a family where her stepmother had locked food away and renamed her and each of her two sisters. My grandmother could not remember her first name, the one with which she was born. She got used to being someone else's, labeled and re-labeled with ownership, like property.

My grandfather kept a chamber pot, a very old-world convenience, which really made no sense in their San Francisco two-bedroom. I lived in that house for a time. When I was eight years old, I was staying with my grandparents and had a fever. In the middle of the night, I made it from the bed through the hallway to the bathroom. How could a grown man not make it ten feet to a proper toilet? Why would he make his wife empty out a pot with his shit and piss?

I think about this often.

She had been renamed Eusebia, but we called her Mama. I'm not sure why we didn't say "Lola," but maybe it was an attempt to leave the Philippines behind. Mama used to watch *General Hospital* while cooking and folding laundry; she'd yell at the TV, which is something I do now. Maybe it's genetic, maybe it's behavior modeling, or maybe it's an attempt to assert ourselves in a world where we feel powerless.

* * *

I know how to keep my head down and do my work.

I know how to make do.

I frequently think, *No, it's ok, I don't really need that.*

I used to never say what I feel; sometimes I still don't, because I know I can continue in spite of not voicing my needs. I always have, and yet here I am.

I'm tired.

I don't want to obey rules that make no sense, to break myself to fix someone else, to diminish my own needs for the good of someone else, to keep the peace.

The only peace I want to keep is my own, but I've never had it, I've never known it.

My existence is literally managing turmoil, surrounded by navigating trauma—both mine and someone else's.

How did this happen?

How is "no" the shortest word and also the hardest to eke out of my mouth?

It's ridiculous and yet totally understandable.

I'm so tired.

My best friend and I sometimes talk about our mothers; they had to suffer, to endure marriages where they were not happy. That was the time period; women didn't get to decide what wasn't working for them and then actually voice it. That idea would break the whole system.

We can't change people; they have to change themselves. I know, at least I highly suspect, that my mother and grandmother thought, *If I can be good enough, if I can be _____ enough, he will be better or treat me better or _____.* It's all conditional, a dance of mysterious cause and effect. It sounds awful, I know it's awful, but maybe I'm doing my own version of it. Dumb shit like how someone cleans the kitchen should not dissolve a marriage, but that's symptomatic of a larger reality: division of labor. Whose time and energy are more valuable? Which person ends up taking care of the one household that serves two (or more) people? Who does the emotional labor, the adulting, the minutiae of daily life? Who gets to live their dream knowing they're always supported; always have backup; and can always get reassurance, answers, entertainment, and love? And who feels like a shadow of themselves?

I'm mean sometimes. It's clearly passive aggression, or some subset of it, this trope of the competent wife and the sometimes-bumbling spouse. Think Homer Simpson or any cartoon or sitcom dad or husband. She knows where things are and what to do in a crisis. He gets jokes and accolades at work. And when they're out on a double date, she notices that when she talks about something that doesn't involve him (it was before they knew each other), he jumps in with his own version of a similar thing.

She took a little bit of spotlight, and he swooped in and took the rest. He didn't realize it. He was uncomfortable.

I was someone before you. I'm still someone now.

So were all our mothers, but when they married and had kids, suddenly they were absorbed into roles they took on without reading the fine print. (The fine print is very, very tiny.) I never asked myself what I wanted, only figured things out by realizing what I didn't want—process of elimination, like they teach us with multiple choice questions on the SAT. There's always a throwaway answer; a right answer; and a trick answer, one that seems right that actually isn't. It's designed to appear correct at first glance, but there's one thing off, one imprecision, one thing that makes it less correct than the real answer. I used to be good at spotting those.

* * *

My anger always has to be dressed, preferably in a costume. It shows up as measured politeness, pre-volcanic calm (that doesn't get to erupt), humor (to spare the other person's feelings), or excruciatingly professional professionalism. It's difficult to move in these getups, these garments. They're both disguise and armor, utilitarian and protective, but also flouncy and distracting. *Yes, I'm mad! But oh no, not really!* I can be upset but not so much that you're uncomfortable. What good would that do?

Sometimes my anger pretends to be a whole other emotion entirely. I once saw a Liza Palmer quote on Instagram, likely from a mindfulness or therapy account, that says, "Anger is just sad's bodyguard."[23] Yes, but why can't anger be an emotion in and of itself, devoid of a connection to sorrow? Is being sad more acceptable than being angry? Is that why I've found myself overwhelmingly sad for so many years?

* * *

There was a time when I punched or kicked a bag and I swear I could feel my brain shake in my skull. It doesn't happen all the time; when I imagine someone's face, someone I don't even want to hurt but who carelessly or thoughtlessly or even unintentionally hurt me, my strikes land differently. I can hear it on impact, the satisfying *whoof* of my fist or shin on leather, my hip turning with the perfect amount of force.

---

23 Guiding Light Counseling (@guidinglight_counseling), Quote by Liza Palmer, *Instagram*, December 15, 2021, https://www.instagram.com/p/CXgd3jfLqwL/.

It's succinct. Unfettered. As precise as a good knife, efficient and spare as a poem.

What if I embraced my anger instead of holding her back until she's wild and flailing?

* * *

A few times in my life, I've had to deal with both unruly children and pets and found my father's voice coming out of my mouth. You haven't seen your trauma on display until you've cussed out a fifteen-pound terrier mix on a public sidewalk. There's a reason I never became a parent; I have the potential to be like my father or worse. My rage would be driven by a lifetime of suppression; I couldn't get angry at him, so having to hold back when no one held back with me—when no one modeled restraint, rationale, empathy—might be impossible.

* * *

One summer, I took a self-defense course and nearly left the last day of class in tears. This wasn't because of anything physical. The instructor was giving some final insights, many students being teachers of martial arts.

"Remember that violence is different for women," he said. "As boys, men roughhouse for play." In other words, they learn violence and aggression in different degrees and contexts. "But women and girls often only experience violence as punishment." That shock of clarity was like having the wind knocked out of me. Being able to control violence and aggression is adjacent to power—the ability to recognize mistreatment, injustice, and dissatisfaction and make demands for changing it. So why would girls and women be allowed *that*? Such power would exalt us; of course the world keeps it from us.

I want to express my anger freely and without apology or self-doubt. However, I don't want the old anger, the fury I've held for as long as I can remember. That's the point: let the anger be ignited, burn, and then burn out until the embers gently fade to ash.

* * *

What will I leave in my wake if I let my anger go?

* * *

Ending 1:

Melanie Hilario was a chronically self-underrated writer, teacher of movement, and human being. She loved to be the hype woman for others because she knew what she often wished she'd had for herself. At some point in her mid-life, she was at a crux, but every path felt like it would lead to a precipice, so she fell into a paralysis of sameness and bland safety. Because she had restrained her fury for so long, it no longer knew how to act. She had forgotten how to protest and push back and set boundaries and then hold those boundaries like a castle gate. She forgot her fierceness. She forgot how to be loyal to herself. She stopped fighting. She stopped caring. She detached. She sublimated herself until she was vapor. Today, she's survived by unfinished chores, unpaid bills, and many blank pages.

Ending 2:

Melanie (Mel) Hilario was a self-proclaimed late bloomer, and true to form, at some point in her mid-life she set her whole world aflame. Not in a burn-it-all-down type of way but rather in glorious supernova fashion. All the excess of her existence fell away into the stratosphere. She wrote, sang, danced, fought, and laughed with abandon. She loved, hated, screamed, cried, and healed. The ghosts of her female ancestors embraced her, sang her to sleep at night, and chanted her name every morning.

When she finally set her anger free, she also freed herself.

A CONTINUOUS
AND WIDENING (OR
TIGHTENING) CURVE

MEL SAAVEDRA

W HAT IS THE LIFE CYCLE OF ANGER? DOES IT HAVE A SHELF
life, or does it flame up and burn out, resolving to ash
. . . only to rebirth itself, to become another version of itself
entirely? Or is it the same long serpent of anger that morphs
and molts, shedding and changing over time, shape-shifting
muscle around the same spine of anger that makes up the
molten center of that rage?

This is a curiosity I have sat with in different ways for
many, many years as the unformed question incubated in my
core, waiting patiently to emerge. Maybe the question had
lain dormant inside me for countless moon cycles. Or, rather
than a curiosity, was it simply an intimacy with anger, a relationship kept in the closet, hibernating underground—the
anger an unseen, unwavering companion—only to come up
out of the earth with eyes piercing into the marrow of me?

In its most potent form, the anger was a nearly imper-
ceptible knot, a burning ember that awoke in me an instinct
to survive—a distinct sensation of being jolted awake—when

I was sixteen years old, faced with either living or simply fading away like an image bleached by the sun. The question has gotten only sharper and more pointed as a grown woman who has survived so much sexual violence and deep emotional abuse, a woman who has spent decades recovering from harm and then committing years to painstakingly transforming into a more whole person, a wholly different version of myself, picking up disparate and scattered parts to piece those shards together. Through this long journey, the anger has always been present, steadfastly loyal.

In that transformation, my relationship to anger and the hostility itself (as it manifested well into my twenties) also mutated; the fires cooled, and the adoption of practices over many years (meditation, breathwork, yoga) rewired neural pathways, rebuilding and strengthening connections that were not only compromised but dismantled and ravaged early on in life.

In some of those early-ish years, starting in my teens, anger fed me, and it was a feast I dove into, starved. The flames nourished me and were also stoked by me, burning me up so I could emerge hardened—at times brittle as I grew and learned through trial and error—fired by the heat.

As I slowly put myself back together again, the anger reflected different dimensions of the person I was discovering, the me I was creating—at turns feisty, reckless, loud, adamant, sensually aggressive, or wildly raucous and in your face. Even as a rough gem, I had a great many sides, and so did my anger. As a woman overcoming a deeply ingrained identity of worthlessness, anger relocated me to other, far less terrified versions of myself, providing a series of portals that transported me away from my trauma to another way of being. It was also, at times, an escape hatch, an easy out to bypass connection with the most painful, ugly parts of myself or others. Yet the anger always eventually provided passage back to the center of my realest self. Anger became my liberation, granting me wings to soar above other people's opinions of me—to soar, oftentimes, above my own opinion of myself, most of all—making me unrecognizable to myself. It was what I thought freedom must feel like, even though that feeling was unknown to me.

Today, I am in a new stage, an entirely different phase of anger's life cycle. For close to two decades now, I have been a parent to a son and a daughter. As a mother of a daughter who has grown into a beautiful young woman, the anger I feel cuts more sharply, more deeply than I (its well-worn companion) could ever have imagined.

The anger is reborn with another life, and me the furious mama bear, snarling, teeth ready to rend flesh in an instant. I feel leagues and leagues away from the calm, tempered woman of maturity I worked endlessly to become from my mid-thirties well into my forties, her anger in hand, reins grasped, intelligent and even graceful in her fury. Because when I feel into the reality for my innocent, dazzling daughter—lovely, sparkling inside and out—and the harm that she's exposed to simply by being, just by breathing—violence that's an impersonal, universal promise of harm—my anger is bottomless, like the depths of the Pacific. It is a mindless wildfire, devouring everything in its path, emotion so enraged it's unspeakable. Simply writing these words has me crying hot, furious tears. And I can feel myself transmute, morphing from a controlled vessel of emotion to an unthinking, sweating, spitting She-Hulk.

My baby girl just turned fifteen. This phase of anger is only just ramping up.

As a woman, what is the legacy I will leave behind for my daughter? What will I teach her by example, as a future ancestor?

At this moment we now find ourselves in the world, I don't yet know the answer. I know some elements . . . many others, not at all. In the brokenness of our societies, our unhelpful archetypes, and the falling apart happening within the depth and breadth of the endless pandemic, I am simply feeling my way through the dark. In the hardest moments, at least, that's how it feels. After forty-eight years of working intimately with anger, years that constitute a lifetime, *will I have the anger or will the anger have me?* I don't know.

So, again, what is the life cycle of anger? There is so much pain in just the question that there is blood in the answer—held silently, daily, sometimes moment to moment, and absolutely breath to ragged breath. Because the burning rage I have felt in my life, looking back on the trauma I have survived, takes on a whole new, massive meaning as a mother with a daughter walking through the world.

One thing I know like I know the sun rises in the east is that I'm a fighter; the women in my lineage, my life experiences, and my spirit have made me so. I will fight no matter what; I will fight to the end, and I will stand up or go down a ferocious woman warrior.

Now, as a protective, fierce mother bear that will decimate whatever is in its path, what is the call that my anger is answering? What does that fire seek to consume? It is a spiral of curiosity that eats me alive some days, bite by bite—much like the anger can—and on other days, it swallows me whole.

THE FIGHT

NICOLE FRANCES WILLIAMS

T HE FIGHT HAS BEEN WITH ME AS LONG AS I CAN REMEMBER, passed down through generations of angry women surviving the hard knocks of angry men. Our bloodlines are swimming with thousands of pieces of broken hearts. Like glass ground to dust, invisible edges of old wounds are a constant source of pain, scratching open fear and regret, snubbing out new lifelines, cutting off new paths. For girls like me, raised in angry houses, The Fight seems impossible to lose, unwilling to rest, too stuck in the flesh to forget.

"I hate this place," I said often of the steadily growing agricultural city that my parents had moved us to the summer before my sixth-grade year. Located on the outskirts of the East Bay Area, it was a place where angry houses hid amid the "normal life" that suburbia promised families like mine who moved there thinking a new house in a quieter town, on a nicer block, down a wholesome street filled with neighborly neighbors was the ticket to a happier life.

In this new place, Mom thought, we could forget about the year before.

* * *

"There's been a report. Neighbors heard screaming," the officer said as my mom stood behind our metal security screen in San Jose, where I grew up before we moved to the place I hated. It wasn't the first time the cops had come to our house, but it was the first time Dad left with them. His head hung low. His hands were behind his back. His eyes were wild.

We lived on a court that crawled up the foothills of Eastside San Jose, close to where Dad had grown up. That meant I had to watch him be escorted by the police down what seemed like an endless flight of stairs to the cop car waiting below. Watching him that day was the first time I remember not seeing my eyes in his, not knowing what he was feeling. But I knew I was angrier than I had ever been before. The Fight was there, boiling in my belly, screaming, "Fuck you!" silently as the flashing lights pulled away, making sure everyone on the street had a chance to see.

I don't remember if I talked to the cops alone that day. I don't remember who called them. I don't remember what I said or didn't say. I don't know if my little brother, Adam, spoke to them too. But I knew Mom must've admitted that he put his hands on her, otherwise they don't take dads away. As I write this now, I'm reluctant to linger too long in the memories I do have of my mom against the bathroom wall. Of me grabbing Dad's hands and arms. Of yelling, "Stop it!" as loud as I could over and over and over again. Of me yelling at Adam to help. Of him sobbing that he didn't know how.

A few months later, Mom started looking for happy houses in happy places. "We need a fresh start," she'd say. And that's how we ended up, the four of us, in this place that I hated.

* * *

Things started off great when we left our angry house behind in San Jose. "This is a safe place to live," my parents said. No more daycare needed after school. They made fast friends with the neighbors. We were invited to barbecues at Tina and Eric's and participated in the strange middle-income tradition of "progressive dinners" where each family hosted one part of the meal, requiring everyone to switch houses after each course. I made friends with the blonde, Christian girl down the street who was also new to town and loved a band called Jars of Clay. She was curious about my Jewish mom and Catholic dad who never took us to church or anything but still believed in God. I was curious about her family who ate dinner at seven o'clock every night and had rules and routines.

At first, the people we met seemed to genuinely like having us around, and both sides of our family visited often. Mom and I would walk around the neighborhood every night to look at landscaping ideas that we could replicate in our yard. My parents worked as a team to landscape and decorate. They laughed a lot and were almost affectionate at times. I thought maybe Dad's domestic violence classes had actually worked.

By the time I was getting ready to go to camp four years later, we were the angry house again: Yelling every day. No more progressive dinners. Fewer invites. I hadn't talked to the Christian girl since our first week of middle school. Dad had stopped going on family trips and golfed all the time.

As June approached the summer before my sophomore year, I was fifteen and going to spend six weeks at River Way Ranch Camp in the foothills of Sequoia National Park. I had been to sleepaway basketball camp the summer before, but this would be a much longer time away. I pretended to be sad to leave my friends and my freshman-year boyfriend, Daniel. Truthfully, I was excited to get the hell away from this place I hated and the broken promise of a fresh start.

Camp promised a chance to be noticed—to be more than The Fight, more than my parents' referee, more than the Mean Sister, more than the Best Friend, more than the Smart Crazy Girl with a life real "good kids" didn't have.

Mom didn't want me hanging around with my "loser friends" all summer, so she researched and found River Way's Counselor in Training (CIT) program, which promised leadership opportunities, resume-builders, and lifelong friends.

"It's perfect for you," she said, showing me the website and adding that it was expensive—thousands of dollars for four weeks. But the best CITs would be offered an additional two weeks "free of charge" to pair up with a real counselor and lead a cohort of campers as they did art projects, horseback riding, jet skiing, tubing, boating, sports, theatrical performances, martial arts, and a whole menu of things I'd never tried.

Now, this is some wholesome shit, I thought to myself. *This is the kind of thing that good kids from good families do during their summer.*

"*Six* weeks will make the tuition worth it," Mom said.

Emphasis on the *six*.

My personal statement for the CIT program deftly detailed my aspirations to go to college and make a difference in people's lives. As always, my prose was impressive and convincing. My grades reflected top marks and advanced courses. I collected required references from babysitting clients, teachers, and my basketball coach, who touted me as responsible, mature, creative, independent, and smart with excellent communication skills, good judgment, integrity, and strong moral character. Each one happily marked the box that said I didn't use illegal drugs or drink.

* * *

A few days before I left for camp, Daniel invited me to Brian's house, where he and his brothers, José and Ryan, and their girlfriends would be hanging out, drinking, and hotboxing the garage. As I walked in and introduced myself to the circle of people passing a plastic bong around, one of the older boys said, "You're too cute to be Daniel's girlfriend." I only knew him as the older guy who had dated one of the dumbest girls in my group of friends. I'd never talked to him, but we'd seen each other at school next to the fence where all the kids who smoked cigarettes congregated between classes.

He smiled at me as I drank my Smirnoff Ice too quickly and took a too-big bong rip. I coughed, my throat burning like a rookie's. The older boy smiled at me affectionately, amused at my inexperience. I could tell from the way he looked at me that he thought I was innocent. I was a good girl in his eyes.

I sat next to Daniel and drank another Smirnoff as I stole glances at the older boy who said I was "too cute." I drank quickly, trying to ease the burning in my throat. Then, I started to get hot and nervous. The room began to spin.

I made it out of the garage without any help and threw up in the bushes outside. Daniel followed me and held my hair back as I tried to get all the alcohol out before Mom arrived. She'd be pissed if she knew I'd drank too much. That wasn't part of the "moderation plan" she and I had discussed before she dropped me off.

"Well, that's really great, Nicole," Mom said when she picked me up. "I wonder what River Way would have to say about this."

They'd probably ask how I got there, I said to myself.

"Mom, I'm fine, I swear," I said, leaning against the passenger side window with my eyes closed. The glass felt nice. "I swear it was just the sugar or something. Just leave me alone." Through the spins and scolding, all I could think of was how nice it felt to be the good girl—even if the older boy was the only one who saw me that way.

* * *

As Mom and I drove to River Way a few days later, I thought about writing my first letter to Daniel. I had no intention of losing my virginity to him, but, nevertheless, I planned to write out explicit sexual desires in the hopes that his brothers and the older boy would read them too. I didn't want to be *too* wholesome, after all.

As we drove, Mom and I brainstormed what my "camp name" would be—an alter ego that every CIT and camp counselor was asked to create in order to keep their real identities secret until the final fire on the last night of camp.

"Maybelline," Mom suggested. (After all, wearing makeup was one of my defining characteristics.)

"No," I said, pulling down the sun visor to look at myself in the mirror, frowning at how bad my skin was under layers of concealer and foundation. "Sounds too girly."

"What about Mac?" I said, suggesting the edgier makeup line for my new identity as I examined the glittery eyeshadow and heavy black eyeliner that I'd chosen for my first day.

When we finally arrived, I was greeted by a host of college-aged, naked-faced counselors.

"What's your name?" asked Summer.

"Nicole," I said.

"No, what's your *camp name*?" she said, smiling.

"She was thinking of Maybelline," Mom interjected.

"No," I said, firmly. "It's actually Mac. M-A-C, like the makeup."

Summer wrote "Mac" in playful letters on a button to pin on my shirt and pointed us to where I could find my room.

In the weeks that followed, I made friends from wealthy neighborhoods in San Francisco and Los Angeles who introduced me to new music and laughed at my stories. Most of the guys referred to me as Mac Truck, ignoring the edgy makeup reference I was going for. "What's that mean, Mack Truck?" I would inquire. They would always reply with something boyish and vague like, "I don't know. Like getting hit with a MACK TRUCK!" and then making big rig noises, "Toot! Toot!"

The Fight I was known for at home—the one that scared good boys my age away—had quieted down, resting for the first time that I could remember. At night, I wrote sexy letters to mail to the older boy by way of Daniel and bonded with the college counselors. Some of the college girls didn't like how much the college guys talked with me. They made catty comments when one of the guys, Scoobie, gave me a neck rub in the clubhouse. They were probably looking out for me the way young women should look out for younger girls. But at the time, I thought they were mean and judgy.

Two weeks in, I stopped wearing makeup. My skin cleared and tanned. I jet skied for the first time, and I paid special attention to the awkward, out-of-place campers—the ones I could tell didn't feel like they quite fit in.

As Mac, I was thriving and confident, and I told Mom as much when I called home.

"That's nice, honey," she'd say distantly. I could tell something was going on, but I tried not to ask. I was feeling good and more certain than ever that going away to college was going to give me a different life—a place where I could reinvent myself like I had done with Mac.

"Where's Dad?" I asked, realizing I hadn't spoken to him since I left for camp.

"Golfing," she said.

"He's golfing a lot," I said.

"Yes, but it's good," she replied. "He's been such an asshole lately. He really embarrassed me at Tina and Eric's house yesterday. Called me a bitch in front of everyone. But don't worry about it. Just focus on having fun."

And for the first time in my life, I did.

Occasionally, however, my mind would wander back to the night before I left for camp.

* * *

"Come sit with me out back," Dad said.

"What's up, Daddyo?" I asked, pulling my knees to my chest as I sat in the patio chair.

"Nothing much, babycakes," he said, his tone much softer than it had been at dinner as he berated my brother Adam for being a sissy momma's boy and Mom for being fat and treating Adam like a baby.

He looked up at the sky and was serious like he always was when we had our special daddy-daughter talks about life and college plans and career dreams and God. I looked at him and thought, *My dad's so handsome*. We shared the same green eyes, big smile, dimples, and wavy hair. It was so easy to see myself in him.

"What do you think of me and your mom?" he asked.

"Mm, I dunno," I said, picking at a scab on my knee. "I think it's like you've always said: stay together until Adam's out of school and then go your separate ways."

When he didn't respond right away and instead looked up at the sky and sighed, cradling the back of his head, I probed, "Why are you asking?" and searched his face for clues and intentions.

"I don't know, baby," he said, rocking in the iron patio chair.

"Well, four more years, Daddy. Then, you and Mom can do whatever you want," I said, holding steadfast to the agreement that was mostly unspoken until now—Mom and Dad would stay married until Adam and I were out of school. "That's what's best for the kids," they'd say.

"Four years is a long time," he said.

"Well, I don't know what to tell you, Daddy," I snapped back. "That's what being a parent is all about. Doing shit you don't want to do." And then I slapped him on the back and mimicked the "tough shit" smile he'd always given me. It was settled. My verdict was in. He smiled and roughed my hair up with his hand.

"My daughter," he said, laughing. "Such a little smart-ass."

"Apple doesn't fall far," I joked and roughed his hair up too.

* * *

After three weeks at camp, I was invited to stay the additional two weeks—six weeks in total. *I made it worth it.* Instead of being over-the-moon proud, Mom simply said she had expected me to get the invitation all along. "You are *my* daughter after all," she said.

Mom, Dad, and Adam were planning to visit me at the four-week mark, so when I saw our light blue Nissan Stanza pull up with no Dad in the passenger seat, I hopped in and asked where he was.

"Golfing?" I joked.

"No," Mom said with the car still in park. "We're getting a divorce."

"Yeah, okay," I snorted, putting my seatbelt on, sitting in Dad's spot. "I'll believe it when I see it." (My parents were perpetually getting divorced.)

"It's different this time," she said.

"Yeah, okay."

"Nicole," Mom said, her voice growing quiet. "He's living with another woman."

My eyes flashed to the rearview mirror, and the truth was there in my brother's dark, sad brown eyes. The weight of all that had broken while I was gone was held in the deep expanses of the quiet place he had made for himself inside. *I never should have agreed to go to camp,* I thought.

"Everything's fine. I'm doing okay. We're going to be okay," Mom insisted all day as she forced us to sightsee and take happy family pictures together, just the three of us. It was like normal—Mom on vacation with just us kids—except Dad was living with The Other Woman.

We stayed in a single hotel room with two beds, Mom and I shared one. When she thought Adam was sleeping, she started to sob beside me.

"What am I going to do?" she cried in a desperate voice I'd never heard before. Where had The Fight in her gone? I wrapped my arms around her, my eyes wide, staring into the dark, my heart beating faster.

"It's going to be okay, Momma," I said softly, smoothing her hair.

I laid there all night, my chest tight and my eyes wide. I clenched my jaw so long it ached, shooting pain up and down the base of my neck to the back of my eyes.

When she dropped me off at camp the next day, I ran to Summer, broke down into tears, and told her everything that had happened. She, of course, had no idea what to say. Summer wasn't some alter ego she'd developed to have a normal life for six weeks. She was a good college girl from a good home and always expected to follow the good path.

And just like that, Mac was gone.

Those last two weeks of camp were a blur. I moved through the motions like all angry girls raised in angry houses are accustomed to doing. I helped out the little kids, smiled, and laughed during the day. At night, I laid awake, surrounded by eight-year-old campers from Beverly Hills, replaying my mom's cry: "What am I going to do?"

Dad came to pick me up alone in his white pickup truck. Like Mom, he assured me everything was okay. As the promise of my summer at River Way disappeared in the rearview mirror, Dad called The Other Woman.

"Talk to Jackie," he said, smiling and shoving the phone in my hands. "You're going to love her."

* * *

In the weeks that followed, my angry life blew up. Mom's eyes changed; her voice strained with hate. Dad refused to get his own place.

"I'm your daughter!" I screamed at him in front of our new house that wasn't new anymore. "I'm begging you, please. I need you to get your own place."

"I can't, babycakes," he said.

"Yes, you can! I'm your daughter. You're supposed to love me more."

When he said nothing, I shouted louder, "Tell me you love me more!" My heart shattered that night on the driveway as I tried to make him see it was *me* he was supposed to choose.

"It's a different kind of love," he said.

"No, I'm your daughter," I gasped and heaved, falling to the concrete, sobbing over and over again, "I'm your daughter. You're supposed to love me more."

"It's just different," is all he would say.

What does a scared, fifteen-year-old daddy's girl do with that?

Fight.

Today, The Fight that got me through is still with me. Together, we picked ourselves up off the concrete the night Dad drove away, refusing to love me more. Together, we escaped angry houses and angry men. Together, we fought against addiction and depression. Together, we made it to college and then to grad school. Together, we traveled the world. Together, we marched and protested and fought for the right for everyone to feel loved by this world. Together, we settled for a fighting kind of love and built the only kind of house we knew how to build—one of anger. Together, we left that house—and my marriage too.

Today, I'm scared, and The Fight is weary. She has been working too long, haunted by ghosts that seem so real but are no longer there, incapable of trust, terrified of care. What am I to do with that now?

Forgive.

SLIPPERY

RACHAEL SIRIANNI

"All of imagination—everything that we think, we feel, we sense—comes through the human brain. And once we create new patterns in this brain, once we shape the brain in a new way, it never returns to its original shape."

—Jay S. Walker[24]

K NOWING THINGS IS MY JOB, AND I MEAN THAT IN A LITERAL sense. I am a scientist who studies the brain. I read about it. I look at it under a microscope. I teach others about it. I probe it, manipulate it, fix it. I contemplate it when I sit in my backyard during quiet moments under the stars. I don't understand it. Does anyone? I wish that someone could be me.

We understand some of it. The brain is an organ that transforms inputs into outputs, and our feelings have a decidedly biochemical basis. There are reasons for our feelings, scientifically observable reasons.[25]

---

24 Jay Walker, "My Library of Human Imagination," filmed 2008, TED video, 6:50, https://www.ted.com/talks/jay_walker_my_library_of_human_ imagination?language=en.

25 Antonio Damasio and Gil B. Carvalho, "The Nature of Feelings: Evolutionary and Neurobiological Origins," *Nature Reviews Neuroscience* 14 (January 2013): 143–152, https://doi.org/10.1038/nrn3403.

I wish to think about anger. The sensation we recognize as anger is triggered by the perception of a threat, typically through a loss of control or autonomy.[26] Anger is often preceded by a familiar emotional milieu involving irritation, frustration, entrapment, or fear. At the level of tissues and organs, anger's primary source involves activation of the hypothalamus and amygdala, regions of our brain that are critical for emotional regulation. This initial stimulus signals the release of a cascade of hormones that produce the physical sensations we recognize as anger. Substances including cortisol, adrenaline, noradrenaline, and norepinephrine raise our blood pressure and heart rate, causing cheeks to flush and palms to sweat in expectation. Our senses are heightened; our muscles tense; the body's stress response is aroused. We are now primed for action and poised to defend ourselves against the enemy.

Anger is a process through which our bodies shut down the rest of ourselves to focus on and resolve a perceived threat.[27] A flood of anger will fundamentally alter cognitive processes, rerouting the way we both perceive and process information, reducing accuracy, precision, and memory.[28]

These scientific explanations are reductionist ways to describe the socio-emotional and biochemical phenomenon

---

26 Robert James R. Blair, "Considering Anger from a Cognitive Neuroscience Perspective," *Wiley Interdisciplinary Reviews: Cognitive Science* 3, no. 1 (January 2012): 65–74, https://doi.org/10.1002/wcs.154.

27 Karja Bertsch, Julian Florange, and Sabine C. Herpertz, "Understanding Brain Mechanisms of Reactive Aggression," *Current Psychiatry Reports* 22, no. 12 (November 2020): 81, https://doi.org/10.1007/s11920-020-01208-6.

28 Eun Joo Kim, Blake Pellman, and Jeansok J. Kim, "Stress Effects on the Hippocampus: A Critical Review," *Learning & Memory* 22, no. 9 (2015): 411–416, https://doi.org/10.1101/lm.037291.114.

of anger. But while observation and measurement are easy, the subjective experience is much harder to define. What we feel is much harder to define. Like anything else, it is context dependent, which means that it can change.

Anger takes charge.[29] Anger is intense. Anger feeds greedily on itself, morphs and multiplies if left unchecked. It is both all-consuming and unpredictable. It may last years. It may last moments.

Anger is an unwanted vagrant. Anger is an army of vagrants rushing through the body to barricade other feelings and dismantle any alternative intention.

Anger is a squid's ink, enveloping the circumstances under which it arose and giving our most primal self the permission to act without restraint.

Anger will overwhelm the mind, blur the sight, and obfuscate recollection.

Fight, or flight? Anger will make you choose.[30]

I have almost no memory of projecting my anger outwardly as a very young child. This perception has been validated by those who knew me at that time. When I was a baby, I did not cry. When I was a toddler, I did not throw tantrums. I was quiet, isolated, generally compliant, and often worried.

One of my most emotionally vivid memories involves a minor incident when I was only five years old. I remember standing in the aisle of an office supply store, my mother just paces away. I was intently focused on a shelf at my eye level

---

29 Paul M. Litvak et al., "Fuel in the Fire: How Anger Impacts Judgment and Decision-Making," in *International Handbook of Anger*, eds. Michael Potegal, Gerhard Stemmler, and Charles Spielberger (New York: Springer, 2010), 287-310.

30 Gadi Gilam and Talma Hendler, "Deconstructing Anger in the Human Brain," in *Social Behavior from Rodents to Humans,* eds. M. Wöhr and S. Krach (New York: Springer, 2015), 257–273.

where a label was turned upside down. I could tell from the numbers that it was upside down, and I was proud of myself for noticing this. Something was wrong, and I wanted it to be right. The solution was simple: I tried to take the label out and put it the right way. But while I had my hands on the tag, the metal hanger slipped, rattling to the ground. The employee speaking with my mother noticed me struggling to fit the piece of metal back on its rack. I felt his reaction to the core of my bones. I remember him striding quickly toward me. I remember his body posture, his towering height, the wrinkle in his forehead, his aggressively red cheeks as he spoke harsh words, and when he asked me what I was doing and told me to stop. I remember his anger.

Anger is unmistakable when you are the recipient. I shriveled into myself, sank into the floor and beneath nothingness. He thought I meant to make his store *messy*. There was the briefest flash of indignation, the momentary outrage I felt over the confusion that surrounded me. But my fleeting anger could not last, and it was rapidly replaced by panic of having misbehaved. Why did my mother not explain that I was good? Why did the adults not know what was inside of me? They thought I was bad. That I did something wrong. My feelings tumbled quickly, tripped over the disorientation of my five-year-old brain until what I felt was transformed into something else. I became consumed by deep-rooted shame over my own incapability. I had not explained myself adequately, and I did not know how. It was all my fault.

Was my feeling of shame better than anger? I would call it preferable.[31] For while anger is about others, shame is about

---

31 Karen Page Winterich, Seunghee Han, and Jennifer S. Lerner, "Now that I'm Sad, It's Hard to be Mad: The Role of Cognitive Appraisals in Emotional Blunting," *Personality & Social Psychology Bulletin* 36, no. 11 (September 2010): 1467–83, https://doi.org/10.1177/0146167210384710.

one's very own self. I can control me, not them. Let it be me, then, not them.

One of the defining features of my anger is that the feeling always fades: within moments, hours, days, or weeks, anger eventually disappears. Can I call its absence a comfort? It is in that moment of physical quiet that I begin to dissect what was. I can see it momentarily, define it, understand it in the way I like to understand things. Anger *because*. Anger *produced*. Anger *revealed*. In that revelation, in the process of understanding, I am changed. Anger is a lever and I am the fulcrum. Anger hurts when it turns on my axis. It calls my attention. It identifies. It destroys. It empowers. I rebuild. And then my anger recedes.

My experience with anger began to grow in complexity and strength as I approached my tween and teen years. I remember fights with siblings and disappointment over rules. I remember intense pain, loneliness, fear, and the near-crushing weight of responsibility. I remember frustration, the oceans of injustice that had to be swallowed or altered into something I could tolerate, something I could live with.

The anger that arises in me may be reassuring in its self-righteous intensity, but it is an unwelcome visitor. I will always wish to evict it.

As I matured, my autonomy to resolve perceived threats also matured. My responses became better defined. More purposeful. Sometimes useful. Anger became a regular part of who I was, a familiar companion, something I could expect as a response from myself and also respond to, something that could be functional as often as it was dysfunctional. I stopped avoiding anger and began to feel it with the rhythm of emotional predictability. Sometimes, my anger would resolve, and with that would come relief.

Anger is a threat without solution, and I cannot live with that. Anger compels me to respond.

But what of the anger that does not resolve? What if I do not respond or satisfy its demands—where does it go?[32] What happens as the feeling rushes through us time and time again as we circle and revisit without relief? It is then that anger does not recede. These biochemicals simmer in our brains and our bodies, mold the clay of our minds against our will, soak us in toxicity and unwilling subjugation to our own dreaded thoughts.[33]

As a young adult, I began to recognize anger as something that must be felt with thoroughness, a tool with which we might shape future actions and feelings. We will be *heard*. We will be *seen*. We will be *validated*. The force of our response changes us. There was an ex-boyfriend: anger was the window by which I recognized our incompatibility. There was a dysfunctional childhood: anger was the motivation that brought me to my field of scientific study. There was medical trauma: anger was the teacher that instilled in me an overwhelming empathy for what I might not understand about others. There was injustice in the world: anger was—and still is—a force through which I step back to make choices that feel right beyond the moment in which I choose them.

Then, there is pain—always pain—often senseless, often pointless, and irrevocably leading me to my own vulnerability.

32 Thomas F. Denson, "The Multiple Systems Model of Angry Rumination," *Personality and Social Psychology Review* 17, no. 2 (November 2012): 103–23, https://doi.org/10.1177/1088868312467086.

33 Agorastos Agorastos and George P. Chrousos, "The Neuroendocrinology of Stress: The Stress-Related Continuum of Chronic Disease Development," *Molecular Psychiatry* 27, no. 1 (2022) 502–13, https://doi.org/10.1038/s41380-021-01224-9.

A thing that lacks purpose is infuriating, and anger can help me deal with that frustration by yielding the appearance of purpose. I choose anger; I am not subjected to it. But anger is not my sword. I do not wield it to harm others on purpose; instead, it is my shield. When I stand behind it, I can ignore my own accountability to understand or change. When I am filled with its sharp intensity, I am transiently strong. When I heed its call, I feel invincible. My blood cools and my heart rate slows as sharp, over-wrought, acidic logic overwhelms me. I am mean. I am specific. I am sure. Who could abandon such certainty in its peak? I seek vindication.

Truthfully, that doesn't feel good, either. Eventually, I always long to escape it.

I am not afraid of becoming angry or of receiving the anger of others. There is a relief in exposing my most urgent needs front and center, raw, unfiltered, and requiring our attention. It is that I am uncomfortable when the emotion does not leave me. I must move instead, make it into something new.

I am angry a lot, and as an adult, I do not hesitate to make my voice or my needs known. This is a skill that I have learned through the recognition that the negativity I feel will not abate until it is processed, until its effects are felt in their entirety throughout my body and mind, and until I have picked and pulled every piece of it out of me.

The visceral memory of anger will always elude my full recollection. For me, anger is unique in this respect. If I bring to mind any other emotion, there is always a flicker of originality, a physical sensation either grounds or directs me. Imagine for a moment the warm, soft weight of an infant in your arms as endorphins rush through tingling fingers: love. The surge of achievement when a long-sought goal is accomplished: pride. The mental tickle of a favorite subject left to roam inside an otherwise quiet mind: curiosity. The physical ache that pierces your core upon loss: grief. The certainty of a choice well made in the face of difficulty: resignation. These feelings wait for us. These feelings may be called upon again and again.

But not anger. Recollected anger is not visceral. Although I know it once existed, I am challenged to truly feel it. There is no intensity. There is no heat. Was I really *that* angry? Was it really worth it? Anger is like the pain of childbirth in that way. I forget, I return, and I do it all over again. How is it that such a profound emotion can be so difficult to access in its full intensity?

Perhaps if I could feel anger at will, anger would lose its bite.

Anger recedes and softens.

Although I suppose it doesn't always. There are some individuals who never get there, some who stagnate without growth, who fail to become comfortable companions with the threats that plague them. Anger allows one to deny culpability, agency, responsibility. To mire in anger is to absolve oneself of accountability for change.

Such denial is not a state I wish for myself.

What does it mean to know anger? The logical flow for what I have written here suggests I should bring us to a satisfying conclusion, a tidy conceptualization.

"Anger should be accepted."

"Anger should be rejected."

"Anger taught me something neat and pretty."

Do I understand anger now? No. I still don't, and I don't like things I don't understand. So, when I feel anger, I will fight. I will fight to define it, fight to understand it, fight to resolve it.

I will fight until my anger becomes something else that I no longer recognize. My anger will slip. It will slip through my veins and my heart. I will feel it until it slips away. Until I can't find it anymore. Until I can't recall.

And that is exactly how I will get through it.

GETTING TO BE ANGRY, LEARNING TO BE HONEST

∧∧∧∧∧∧∧∧∧∧∧

STEPH STERN

I N MY FAMILY, IT WAS OKAY TO GET ANGRY, TO YELL, TO BE IN A funk, and to slam your bedroom door in fury. So many people, especially girls, learn at a young age that their anger isn't welcome. But anger *was* welcome in my home. Growing up, my mom made sure that my sister and I knew that it was okay for women to get angry. It was okay to explode, especially within the safe confines of our nuclear family. Getting angry at someone didn't mean you loved them any less; in fact, I got the message that you only got to be so angry and yell at the people who most loved you. And we did get angry, especially my older sister, who would frequently slam her bedroom door in frustration.

In retrospect, anger was a tool in our family to get your way. It worked in a family that was very loving but had no skills to negotiate needs, little comfort with self-reflection, and few mechanisms for talking through problems. An outburst of anger meant that everyone else caved in to the needs and wants of the person who was losing it. We accommodated the immediate demand to resolve the intensity of the anger and disconnection it caused and brushed everything else aside without discussion. There were never any grudges for having been shouted at; it was almost like it never happened. That was our family norm.

Because of this, I can get angry. Like when, at an earlier job, I had a boss who frequently got heated. He never exactly yelled, but he could be forceful and intense. Many of our colleagues shut down, froze, and went silent, but my instinct was to match him. It was the conflict pattern we were both used to: we had a basis of mutual trust and respect, so a bit of heated argument was ok. I took pride in not shutting down and being able to stand up for myself and for my peers when this boss overreacted.

I think this is exactly what my mom had in mind. My mom didn't want anger to be the domain of men. She didn't want us to be pushovers. My mom came of age in the sixties and worked as the third female reporter at the *Wall Street Journal* in the seventies. This was her second-generation, feminist perspective: we, too, could be like the men. She all but refused to buy us Barbie dolls and made sure that we had a cowboy set to play with—gun, holster, and all.

Although I could hold my own, I also learned that it didn't feel good to get angry and get my way. As a kid, I was painfully shy and rewarded for being sweet, easy, and helpful. I see now that I had few ways of expressing my needs and was afraid of asking for what I wanted. I'm not sure I even *knew* my wants and needs; it was almost always easier to just go with what my older sister wanted. I see now that my real preference was to be seen and considered by my family. Eventually, I would blow up over an accumulation of these unrecognized, unmet needs. I'd end up angry over something small, like going to the park in the afternoon or what we ate for lunch. While my family capitulated to my demand and I got what I wanted, any lingering feelings of anger were immediately chased away by regret.

Harriet Lerner, therapist and author of *The Dance of Anger,* writes, "Anger is a tricky emotion. It signals that something is wrong but it doesn't tell us what is wrong or how to approach the problem in a growth-fostering way that leads to lasting change . . . . Often we march off to battle without knowing what the real issue is, or even with whom the real issue is."[34] My family's accommodation only took care of the immediate demand (the park, the lunch), and never what led up to it, never clearing the accumulation of feeling unconsidered. I didn't care anymore about the park or the lunch and had no understanding of any deeper need.

I imagine this angry, fiery part of me that marches off to battle as a little girl wielding a huge sword, one at least twice her size. Afraid of overreacting, she only comes out after having been ignored for a while. When she launches into battle, the timing always feels a bit arbitrary. In retrospect, I had learned that anger was a last resort. Before that, it was best to shove frustration down and be easy going. Because of my mom's insistence that anger was welcome for us girls, because I knew that I could get angry, I didn't see how much I also avoided my anger. I never thought to do anything differently, to look at the patterns or plumb for anything in the depths under the anger. I never thought to understand this little girl with her big sword.

---

34 "What Selling 3 Million Copies of 'The Dance of Anger' Has Taught Renowned Psychologist Harriet Lerner," Kathy Caprino, April 23, 2014, https://www.forbes.com/sites/kathycaprino/2014/04/23/what-selling-3-million-copies-of-the-dance-of-anger-has-taught-renowned-psychologist-harriet-lerner/.

It took me ten-plus years of therapy to honor this little girl. Even so, I can still get angry in this same childhood pattern, only more subtly. One time, just once, I yelled at my partner. It was an angry explosion that was so normal in my family. I wish I could remember what it was that I was so angry about. It was early on in our close-to-ten-year relationship, so I imagine that it wasn't so much what was driving the anger but the underlying fear that he wasn't fully into me. Whatever it was, my lid was flipped, and my prefrontal cortex was offline. I have no memory of the content, just the aftermath of him curled up in bed clutching the covers to his chin, shaken and shut down. I felt terrible, monstrous, like a kid that fries ants with a magnifying glass and is then horrified at the massacre. I've never done it again. I do get frustrated at him, angry even. But I've never again shouted like that.

My anger was unacceptable to both of us. In couple's therapy, we worked on our conflict styles. We learned to appreciate each other's defense mechanisms (my anger and him shutting down). We understood that we were both just being self-protective in the ways we had learned in our youth. I learned to ask for my needs more quickly.

"When you're feeling disconnected, do you think you just need to share how you're feeling?" This was obviously a leading question from our therapist, but she was right. My attempts to connect by prodding my avoidant partner were not successful and left me feeling alone and, when left to fester, turned to anger. Being easy leads to being angry.

I learned how to express my emotions differently and, most importantly, to catch smaller frustrations earlier before it all boils over. We can joke about it more too, like when I was recently feeling annoyed at him about something, and I got to tell him that my little girl was upset and wanted to poke him with her sword! I poked him jokingly a few times on the arm, which cooled the intensity of the frustration. Because I had found some more workable tactics, I again didn't see how much I was still avoiding my anger.

* * *

Because of my family pattern of anger at home and politeness with strangers, I've often had the experience of quietly listening to a white man talk at great length while I secretly want to explode. Though I got the message as a kid that girls can be angry, I didn't learn that girls can take up space. The force of culture was too strong, my position as the younger sibling led to shyness and discomfort with too much attention.

When it happens that men take up so much space, my anger starts slowly. First, there's a thought that seems more like mild annoyance, then heat builds in the chest and arms. There's a sense of being trapped. I can't leave—too rude, too impolite. I feel like I'm overreacting and that I can't be angry at this person that I barely know. Instead of being honest, I'm easy. I smile and nod.

In my mind, though, I sometimes imagine cutting him to pieces, letting my little girl take her big sword to him and him comically falling away in chunks. This is how I recently dealt with another angry male colleague. I would sit in meetings with this man (let's call him Jim), angry, and I would let that little girl with the big sword—in my imagination—hack this guy to pieces. Then I'd respond from that other part— the polite, warm professional side. "I see you're upset, Jim. Let's explore this, I want to make sure I understand." I aimed for faux empathy.

To Jim's credit, he was aware of his own anger. He responded well when others expressed their anger and frustration. It meant he wasn't the only difficult one with all the emotions; we were in it together. It was a lesson in anger as a source of connection, which surprised me. Although, why was I surprised? Honesty of emotions and their experience is the true source of connection. Over the course of our project together, I learned to give more voice to my feelings. Even so, I never got to a sense of parity; when I look back, I wish I had expressed even more. I wish I had been more honest.

* * *

I want to outgrow that childhood duality of being easy or being angry, into a place of honesty. But if I'm being honest with you, I'm afraid of anger. Anger is powerful and destructive at times. When I think back to being a kid, the idea of my parents' anger is terrifying. They are as tall as giants and truly scary when angry and yelling when I imagine them from my little kid perspective. Yes, I learned I could fight fire with fire, but there's fear there too, and more of it than I had realized.

Because of this fear, there are so many ways I cage and squash my anger. I don't want to be angry. I judge it ("I shouldn't be angry"), I diminish it ("I'm not angry, just *a bit frustrated*"). I stuff it down. I rationalize. I breathe. I avoid. I'm embarrassed by how it can explode, blow-torching people around me. That's no way to treat a loved one, especially when I spend so much time meditating and going to therapy! Especially when I professionally coach others to learn about *their* feelings! I didn't see how much I was still resting on old ways of diminishing my own needs, playing nice and being easy. If I don't need anything from my partner, if

I can take care of everything on my own, then I don't need to get angry. If I can do the work to update my story and turn around my narrative, then I don't need to be angry. I hadn't seen how much work I was putting into not exploding by not even needing anything.

This doesn't mean I never explode anymore. Just a month or so ago, my partner and I were walking in our neighborhood and chatting about upcoming plans. I was ready to start planning a big trip to visit my family for the December holidays. His immediate response was that if a job came up, he would take it. He's a freelancer and doesn't know his schedule more than a few weeks in advance. I already had a lot of pent-up frustration over the challenges of scheduling. That day, those feelings boiled up, a surge of energy and force rising out of my chest, heating my cheeks. If I'm being honest, it wasn't just about the holiday plans; I was angry because I felt powerless. His work schedule demands that I be flexible or make plans without him. He has canceled on a family trip entirely and joined halfway through another. If I'm being honest, under the anger is sadness and disappointment.

So, my anger exploded on the street that day, but I didn't explode *at* him. I felt the flare of energy as a big lurch. "I'm having a big reaction," was what I managed to say. I could be with my anger, breathe with it. I recognized its force as a protective one. Anger was asking me what I'd been suppressing—the sadness and disappointment that had been accumulating, unspoken. I'd wanted to be independent, to be supportive of his work, not to make him feel guilty. I wanted to be easy. We talked through it in a way that satisfied the anger and spoke for the sadness, at least enough for that day. I was honest with him; I was honest with myself.

These days, I get excited about women's anger. I'm more curious about my anger, more inviting of the force of its passion—a necessary and often appropriate response in a world that wants us to stay easy. When I set out to write, I was hoping my anger would be forged into the type of anger that tears down systems of oppression, that speaks the truth, that doesn't need to be liked. Instead, this process has been humbling. I see how deep the roots of being easy are in my system. When I can be with that little girl with her big sword, anger burns my excuses, my avoidance, and my fake politeness, and I can start to explore the reasons behind it. Anger is a harbinger of deeper needs but no longer my only tool for making myself heard. Anger gets to play a more mature role—to bring a new clarity and help me recognize there's something more true to be spoken.

COMING OF ANGER

∧∧∧∧∧∧∧∧∧

TIFFANY PHAM

Trigger warnings: suicidal ideation and sexual trauma

I'VE LIVED IN A CONSTANT STATE OF FIGHT OR FLIGHT MY whole life. Growing up, anger was all around. My dad was very angry, my older brothers were angry, Mom had moments of anger, and I was angry too. Anger was such a default emotion in my home that I didn't even know why I was angry most of the time, but I cried, yelled, and acted out. Toward middle school, I became destructive and began various forms of self-harm. I remember wanting to hurt myself, even contemplating suicide. I'd light fireworks and let go at the last second—part of me hoping to get hurt and the other part of me afraid. I cut myself a few times but never too deep. I wanted so badly to escape and feel something other than the pain of anger. But this isn't a sob story, it's a coming-of-anger story.

I was never taught healthy coping skills. When Dad would yell at Mom, she would do whatever she could to appease him. It seemed like she wasn't fazed by his anger. He was the only one providing for our family, so we were supposed to accept his anger and be grateful. I've come to understand that Dad's anger was fueled by being the sole provider for our family, working seventy-plus hours a week, and taking care of his mom and sister after losing his dad at a young age. All of that was on top of the trauma of escaping the Vietnam War. Like me, he was also constantly living in fight-or-flight mode. My parents unconsciously modeled to me that anger will get you what you want, and you shouldn't worry if it affects other people.

They also taught me to avoid hard feelings with anger and blame. "Sorry" was not a part of our family's vocabulary, and there was no such thing as regulation or reconciliation. When my brother was a teenager, my parents bought him a giant bag of rice so he could punch out his anger instead of leaving holes in our walls. This taught me to get physical with my anger too by slamming doors, throwing things, or snapping a rubber band on my wrist. It seemed like all these destructive habits felt better than being with anger. I wanted to run away from these intense emotions because being with them deepened my sense of loneliness.

Growing up Vietnamese American and the youngest of three with nearly a decade in between us, I never felt understood by my family. With the age gap, it was almost like growing up as an only child. I was around eight when my parents took me to Disneyland for the first time. My dad proclaimed himself "too old" to go on the bigger rides with me, and Mom said they gave her a headache. I was in the happiest place in the world with my parents, but it felt lonely. I was so mad that I didn't get to go on the rides I wanted, and I was even madder that my brothers had enjoyed Disneyland together when they were my age. If I had been closer in age to my brothers, I could've gone with them, or my parents would've been younger and could've gone on the rides with me. This anger felt justified; after all, I hadn't asked to be born late.

As I developed relationships outside of my family, I felt less alone but grew an addiction to validation. In elementary school, my mom wanted to avoid after-school traffic, so she would pick me up thirty to forty-five minutes late. I learned to befriend my teachers and help out around the classroom to pass the time. By fifth grade, I wanted to stay after school even later because I had found a connection with my teachers and a purpose in helping them out. This desire continued through middle school; I became an office and teacher's assistant during my elective classes. The faculty loved me, which made me feel validated and less lonely. Then one day, as I went to choir class to drop off an office note to a student, a friend excitedly said my name aloud and other kids joined in. That moment showed me that it felt even better to be validated by my peers than by adults.

One of my close friends at the time, who we'll call Carrie, took me to Hawaii with her family in the seventh grade. Carrie's family had a timeshare in Hawaii, so she went there a couple of times a year and made friends with some locals. When we arrived, she introduced me to them—one of the guys she was hooking up with, his friends, and some new people she didn't know yet. As someone who was craving connection and validation, this was a dream come true for me, though in hindsight, I can see how this trip instilled additional toxic coping mechanisms like drinking and dissociating. I drank for the first time ever and inadvertently blacked out into a pool of my own vomit. This trip was also the first time I was hit on, and by multiple guys too. They all happened to be older, and some had girlfriends already. Cue me learning that male validation felt even better than peer validation.

Fast forward to high school, when I realized it wasn't male validation I actually longed for; it was female. I remember having a crush on a girl as early as preschool, but I didn't fully realize my queerness until I actually began dating girls senior year. Looking back, it seems like the more I dated, the more intense my anger got. The stakes grew higher as I grew more invested in the relationships. The fights got more severe and heartbreaking. I couldn't tell you what all the fights were even about, but there were many. With my first girlfriend, we had a big fight where I was crying and running out of her house in the middle of the night—not sure where I was running to, just wanting to run away from the pain. This was the same yearning for escapism I'd felt when I was younger. My dating life became the primary source feeding my addiction to validation and, as a result, my anger as well.

I loved the attention and validation from girls so much that I often dated multiple girls at once, something that I'd learned was acceptable back in Hawaii. This inevitably got me in trouble, of course. A rock-bottom moment for me was when two of my exes began dating each other. I was absolutely gutted—it felt like a personal attack on me. I was devastated and livid at the same time. It was double the rejection, with the cherry on top being them choosing each other instead. Sure, you could say it was my karma for dating them both and going back and forth, but it still hurt, nonetheless.

You would think I learned my lesson, but if anything, it taught me not to get so invested. It taught me to date around or just hook up instead of being in a relationship, which was great! I could soak in all the female validation I wanted without getting hurt, right? Wrong. I eventually fell back into a relationship and got slapped in the face—or genitals rather—with an STI—HSV-1, or oral herpes spread genitally. Another rock-bottom moment for me. I thought my life was over, that no one would ever want to touch me again. My sadness was met again with anger and blame. I was so mad at my girlfriend for giving me this virus I'd have for the rest of my life.

How did she not know she had herpes? Why would she be intimate with me if she knew something was off?

When I told my parents about the STI, Dad was surprisingly chill about it. Mom, on the other hand, was livid. She yelled at me and asked why I would do something like that, as if I had a choice. She said some terrible things about my girlfriend and that she knew I shouldn't have been with her. Once again, she resorted to blame instead of regulating her anger. Even though, too, had blamed my girlfriend, what I really needed from my mom was love and compassion.

A week later, my mom hired a massage therapist to come to the house, Jack Lopez. This massage was life-changing in the worst way possible. Jack groomed, manipulated, and molested me that day and the handful of additional times that I saw him from 2013 to 2015. I didn't fully understand that it was assault at the time, though. I had recently gotten herpes and thought no one was ever going to want to touch me again, yet here this person was touching me. It wasn't until ông ngoại, my grandfather on my mother's side, passed away that it finally registered. After ông ngoại's funeral service, Jack was hired to come to my uncle's house and massage the family. That was the last time he molested me and the first time he molested my younger cousin. I immediately knew what happened when she came downstairs and said, "Well, that was different." It took him violating another family member for me to register that what he had done to me all along was wrong. Despite finally realizing the abuse, I still didn't speak up, not even to my younger cousin. Five years went by without thinking about any of this until a similar energy resurfaced in my next relationship. We'll call her Paula.

When we first met in 2014, we were instantly enamored of each other. It was the healthiest relationship either of us had had. For the first time, I felt unconditional love and experienced better communication than ever before. In hindsight, I can also see the vast amounts of projections occurring on both ends and how codependent we were. I loved her so much, and yet I'd find myself yelling at her in a similar way that Dad used to yell at Mom and the rest of us. I never wanted to embody that. When I made the connection that my anger was as awful as my dad's, I felt so out of control. Here I was filled with awareness of my anger, but I still couldn't help it; my anger had a mind of its own.

It makes me sad to think about the way I projected my emotions onto Paula, because I know exactly how it feels to be on the other side of anger. It hurts in a complex way, where I am both the victim and perpetrator. No one ever says, "I want the bad qualities of my parents," but unfortunately, it's not something we get to choose. While I wasn't conscious of this choice while we were together, I now know I get to choose if I want to continue perpetuating these bad qualities or not.

Paula often stayed silent and appeased me to resolve our fights, similarly to how Mom did with Dad. Then we trivialized my behavior by referring to it as when I'd go "Asian dad" on her, as if my anger was a disease that couldn't be helped. We also became really good at forgetting and moving on. There wasn't a ton of regulation or reconciliation, which was, again, similar to my family's dynamic. After the honeymoon phase of our relationship, we started having intimacy challenges. I remember Googling, "why don't I want to have sex with my girlfriend?" The situation was confusing because I used to love hooking up, and there were still moments when our sex life was great. While this seemed like an issue, it also felt workable and wasn't enough to stop us from getting engaged in 2019.

It was Labor Day weekend of 2020 when Paula came on to me, and I finally had a lightbulb moment. At some point, the energy of her wanting me transitioned from extreme validation to me feeling like a vampire's victim. The feeling became similar to when Jack took advantage of me. My whole life, I had been craving connection, but I started to learn that, when the connection lacked consent, it didn't feel right. It feels silly to even write that, like it should be obvious, but that's another thing I'm learning—that nothing is obvious. I thought that when you were in a relationship with someone, consent was a given or that both parties would magically be on the same page. When I realized this consent piece, it explained my resistance to intimacy with Paula—her assumptions felt like a lack of consent.

While I wasn't ever able to say "no" to Jack, I was finally able to say "no" to my fiancée. This put us in a trauma loop; my "no" was perceived as rejection and triggered her fear of abandonment. I felt like she didn't understand my pain or boundaries, and she felt like I didn't love her. We had weekly check-ins with each other and biweekly couple's coaching to remedy the relationship. While we were both exhausted from all the emotional labor, it felt like progress was made. I had no idea she was going to break up with me on the evening of her birthday in 2021. I felt so blindsided and abandoned. My initial reaction was a defensive, "well if you don't want to be with me, then fine" type of energy. I cycled through all the stages of grief. I was so angry that she didn't bring this up sooner—why now and out of nowhere? We continued with couple's coaching through our decoupling process, which was really helpful, especially in figuring out how to manage time with our dog, Joey, who we had adopted a year prior.

We both love Joey so deeply. Paula got an emotional service animal letter from her therapist, so she felt connected to Joey in a prescribed way. We adopted Joey together and jointly decided to put my last name on her collar, so I felt like she was a part of me. When I moved out of the place we shared together, we agreed Paula would be Joey's primary parent until I found my footing. Once I did, I was sporadically allowed to see Joey until we agreed that I could have Joey once every other weekend, because a week was too long for Paula to be without her. At this point, Paula had decided to remove my last name from Joey's collar. As frustrating as this all was, I still had so much love for Paula and empathized with her. The tables had turned, as I was now appeasing her. My anger went dormant out of shame because part of me could see that Paula's selfish actions were the result of the damage my anger caused in our relationship.

At the end of 2021, Paula told me that the back-and-forth coordination with Joey was too hard for her, and she needed a three-month break. My anger escaped from hibernation and thought, *Thank God we didn't have kids together; she can't even manage to share custody of our dog!* I accommodated her again with the contingency that we would regroup after her respite and figure something out together. However, when the break was over, she said she was keeping Joey, and time would tell when we could talk again. My anger became rage. I was heartbroken, livid, and somehow still sympathetic. I was confused about how we had gotten here, how Paula went from my fiancée to a complete stranger. I felt betrayed because we had an agreement that was all of a sudden met with, "I changed my mind." Yet, I still had compassion for her because, deep down, I wanted to believe she didn't mean to hurt me like I never meant to hurt her. Part of me even wanted to celebrate her for standing up for what she needed.

I've yet to hear from Paula and don't expect to for a while, but I'm choosing to accept what I cannot control. I can't wait until the day I see Joey again, but I also know she's a part of me, whether she's physically with me or not. I'm choosing to no longer be in a codependent relationship with Paula. I choose to validate myself and not let her actions or words dictate how I feel, just like how what happened with Jack doesn't define me either. I'm choosing to be a survivor instead of a victim.

It's taken a lot of healing, therapy, and time for me to process the sexual trauma, come to terms with the abuse, and share my story. I only recently learned that Jack's massage license was suspended in 2017 for five years due to his 2016 conviction of second degree assault and two counts of fourth degree assault with sexual motivation. I was filled with both relief and anger. His license was only suspended for five years? Those five years are already up now. Can he get a license again after everything he's done? Hearing that there were other survivors brings me comfort in knowing that I wasn't alone in my experience, and at the same time, it makes me wonder if I could've saved them by speaking up sooner. If I could've saved my younger cousin . . .

Through my healing journey, I've learned why I kept going back to Jack's massage table, beyond the coincidental timing of my STI. Somewhere along the road, with a lot of professional help, I made the connection that 2013 wasn't the first time I was molested. When I was around five years old, someone else touched me inappropriately, ironically or not, in a massage setting as well. This imprinted the programming that led twenty-three-year-old me not to immediately sound the alarm bells that something was wrong with Jack. I'm still healing this part of me, but the clarity and connections have been instrumental in my repair process. It's made me realize that anger will always be a part of me and not to be ashamed of it anymore, while also not letting it consume me.

My anger has always been present in relationships with other people, always directed toward and often blaming my family, partners, or Jack. Now I'm choosing that anger be in relationship with me. I'm tired of being a victim to other people and external factors that I cannot control. I know I can only control my own actions, boundaries, and voice. So here I am expanding, opening, and ready to listen to what anger has to teach me. Is it another boundary being crossed? Is it an ancestral wound longing to be healed? What's wanting to be tended to? Whatever it is, I'm committed to building my relationship with anger so I can regulate, reconcile, and connect with myself.

THE UPWARD SPIRAL

YOLANDA MARIN-CZACHOR

THE FURY BEGAN AS A MINOR PINCH OF THE DIAPHRAGM. I took a breath and it traveled toward my chest, heating my torso and numbing my shoulders. The next inhale and my head was pounding while my scalp tightened. I wanted to scream in frustration and fear, but it was morning and my toddler lay nearby, blissfully asleep. I looked wildly around the room, as if the cure would somehow reveal itself to me. There was nothing. Just me, my baby, my helplessness, and the screaming in my mind.

I'd just received a diagnosis the day before flying to Central America to visit family. At the time, I was relieved to have answers for the constant pain. But I figured there was plenty of time to process it while I was away. I would get through the trip, give my daughters a good time, and visit some sites while I digested the diagnosis and planned my strategy. Two mornings later, I silently raged against a foreign bedroom floor, furious that I couldn't seem to hold up the weight of my own body. My throat ached with resentment.

I'd been so stoic throughout a high-risk pregnancy, a complicated birth, and a high-needs preemie. I'd managed it while raising my four other kids because I was determined to keep the household running despite my aches and pains. For most of my life, my willpower had been an ally. I believed that if I just lasted a little longer, tried harder, or worked smarter, I could meet my goals. I knew what I needed in order to complete tasks, and I often succeeded.

So, what happens when your body gives out? What if your body decides that no matter how much you're willing to endure, no matter how hard or intelligently you yearn to work, you can still wake one gorgeous morning and collapse onto the floor? Your legs become useless, your arms feel heavy, your mind is underwater, and all your thoughts are distant and muffled. You thought you had more time. You thought you'd find the solution. You were so wrong, and all you can do is clench your jaw with fury at your own body as you try to climb back onto the bed.

I was never an athlete. I wasn't the most coordinated team player, either. Yet, I always had an incredibly intuitive connection to my body. I sensed when something was off, and I knew what I needed to alleviate a pain or discomfort. If I decided to get into shape, I accomplished it. If I had to pull an all-nighter, I knew my dependable body would get me through the night and produce beautiful results. Whip up a holiday party for fifty people while handling a newborn? Piece of cake. My confidence about many things may have wavered, but I never doubted my physical abilities until my body gave out one sunny morning.

Years would pass as I grappled with my new existence. A new diagnosis would be added to the original, and more physical pain and incapacitation would come with it. Infusions, pills, therapies, diets, hospital stays, canes, and forced bed rest. But when I was asked how I managed it, I never spoke of the anger that clawed at my chest at night when insomnia was in control.

"Think positively. It could be worse. You are fortunate. This isn't such a big deal." I played this litany in my head to the pulsing beat of my inflamed and tender joints. I needed to focus and work harder on healing myself. That was my only goal—to find remission. So, I hastily stifled the fear and betrayal and launched myself into everything I could find in an effort to win the battle with my immune system. I battled for years.

The day of my complete unraveling arrived on yet another lovely morning as I struggled to lift my arms to shampoo my hair. The steam of the shower was dizzying, the effort of wrapping a towel around myself caused spots to float across my eyes. I stumbled toward my bed, heart pounding, covered in sweat, and hands trembling. I shoved my face into a pillow and screamed and screamed until the tears came. It was all so futile. Anger is often a reaction to fear or grief, and I was overcome by both as my body broke our contract. My ally was now an adversary whose language I didn't speak. I seethed with the injustice of it. What was I to do if I couldn't be useful to my loved ones? How could I live with illnesses that would make me reliant on others for help? I collapsed against the sheets as all my strength, all my willpower, deserted me. I was stripped, bare, exposed as nothing more than a shell of who I'd once been. I was powerless, and I cried out that I'd finally given up.

The wise Buddhist nun Pema Chödrön once wrote: "Begin the journey without hope of getting ground under your feet. Begin with hopelessness."[35]

---

35 Pema Chodron, *When Things Fall Apart: Heart Advice for Difficult Times,* (Boston: Shambhala Publications, Inc., 2000), 56.

I was quite intimate with the feeling of the ground, and there was no way that I was going to lift myself off of it—on my own—that day. As I lay in a heap, shattered by my grief and rage, how could I have known that this unraveling would begin my journey out of the dark? I had nothing left in me, so I reached out and asked for help. My independence warred with my reality, and I struggled not to sink into bitterness as my husband covered me in blankets and assured me that I'd be fine. How in the hell would I be fine?

Days became weeks and tears dried: fear retreated as my mind gradually adjusted to each change in my system. I'd develop a new pain, and I'd begin to panic once again, but I'd remember to breathe, to wait. It passed, and I learned. All pain—no matter how foreign and new—eventually abated. I'd release a hoarse sigh of relief as I slipped into a bone-weary sleep.

A new emotion began to replace the anger that I'd grown accustomed to when things went wrong. There was a hush, a stillness that I'd never allowed inside my cluttered brain. When one's body is not cooperating and one's emotions have run their course, there's only silence left. I lay within that quiet space for weeks, listening to the cars pass my home and the rain patter on my windows. I heard dogs bark, children laugh, the faint murmurings of the television in another room as I waited for the frustration to return. It didn't, and I was bored, so I began to read. And read. And read.

For most of my life, I'd patted myself on the back for my fortitude in the face of conflict. I dismissed the notion that I needed to deal with my past, that I was still affected by the grief of all that I'd lost as an orphaned child. I was raised as a tough, stoic New Yorker, not a wilting flower. I was dependable and unwavering. I'd been a single parent for years, and

I'd single-handedly protected my eldest daughter from harm within the constraints of an intimidating and loud city. Hell, I'd once fought off an attacker with a sharp elbow and well-placed stiletto. There was nothing that I couldn't accomplish with a strong cup of coffee in one hand and some power pumps on my feet. Why reflect when you're invincible?

To my bemusement, I learned that the hours of solitude that I spent in my room were a meditation of sorts. Without the ability to accomplish and conquer, and with the grief and fear silenced, my mind was emptied of most of its tasks. So, I sat and listened. My youngest daughter's juicy giggles made me smile, and my husband's rich voice softened my heart. I went inward and examined years of suppressed traumas and a painful childhood of violence and loss. I sat with those memories, sifting through the countless moments of oppression and hostility. I saw that child retreat with each scream, each splintered piece of furniture, every shattered bottle and stale cigarette that littered the sticky surfaces of her life. And yes, I railed against the unfairness of a world that would tarnish innocence and hope to such an extent that the physical body would simply collapse three decades later.

There are times when the body is wracked with crashing waves of such agony that there's no time to swim to the surface. You gasp for air and a new surge smashes you against rocks. You flail as you wait for a break in the tumult, but a larger swell engulfs you. You wonder if this one will finally pull you under, and you cry out with helplessness and terror once again. But always, always, that moment of peace returns. And each time that happens, you remember that there's no need to fight. You get better at relaxing your frightened body, allowing it to drift from harm. You surrender to the process long enough and you eventually find the shoreline again.

One morning, my husband woke me with my usual cup of coffee, and I opened my eyes to his profile as he gently lay the mug on my nightstand. I was captivated by the softness of this gruff man's demeanor, by the kindness in his profile as he tended to his wife without complaint. A rush of gratitude washed over me, and something in my broken heart clicked into place. Gratitude. It was gratitude that would drive me toward love. How fortunate I was to have someone's kindness to greet me in the morning. How lucky that he drove me to my numerous appointments without hesitation. Later that day, I sat on someone's couch, and I spoke of all my losses and anger with a candor that I'd never allowed of myself. I looked across the room into a virtual stranger's caring eyes, and I was once again awash with thankfulness for the compassion that this soul extended to me.

I continued to reach inward and outward. I found loving people who committed themselves to help me unearth and examine the detritus of a life that I'd kept locked behind a vault of sheer willpower and obstinance. I released pride, and with it, I was given a new understanding. What's stronger than anger and fear? What can overcome both the anguish of a tormented past and the anger of such a painful present? Love does. Love for others, love for oneself. Love for the moments between the pain. I began to understand this, but still, I struggled with the process.

This is how my journey took a turn from helplessness to growth. This is when I understood that even in the most brutal and crushing pain, there is a lesson to be learned. A lesson of resilience, of courage, of love. I have been on my knees for much of this journey, and I have learned that to reach out and receive is the greatest gift. And with every quivering step I take, I am thankful. How else could I have learned how beautiful it is to merely breathe in life, to cherish the simple comfort of a soothing bath, to welcome the smile of a helper as they extend their hand?

And so, I walk this path of chronic pain with all of my imperfections and setbacks. I honor the frustration and anger on the rare occasion that they still visit me, letting the feelings wash through me as I focus on each breath. Sometimes, the heat rises, and I clench my fists against the inconvenience of this exhaustion. Other times, the tears come. They are all reminders that I'm human and that my journey is less linear and more of a spiral upwards as I find myself returning to love. Always, always, it ends with a tenderness for all I've accomplished and for all I've been given.

There are nights when insomnia reminds me that I'm not in control of my body or its demands, and I make myself still as I allow the darker emotions to work their way through me. I sift and weigh them, I examine and turn them over in my mind, asking myself how they are there to serve my healing journey. Some are there to strengthen my resolve, some are there to show how far I've come, others remind me of what still remains before me. I even whisper to them in the darkness on some nights. We speak of our path together, of our once bloody and chaotic narrative, and of the stories of triumph that we wish to tell one day. I murmur gently to the anger and fear that this will be brief, and morning will always come, carrying hope and opportunity in its wake. I turn my face toward the light that awaits me; I think of the fondness that I have for my brave body as it faces its struggles with tenacity and courage.

After all, it is often our intimacy with the darkness that allows us to revel in the light.

BIBLIOGRAPHY

4-H. "4-H Homepage." Accessed July 13, 2022. https://4-h. org/.

Agorastos, Agorastos, and George P. Chrousos. "The Neuroendocrinology of Stress: The Stress-Related Continuum of Chronic Disease Development." *Molecular Psychiatry* 27, no. 1 (2022) 502–13. https://doi. org/10.1038/s41380-021-01224-9.

Beach Boys. "Surfer Girl." Track 1 on *Surfer Girl*. Capital Records. 1963.

Bertsch, Karja, Julian Florange, and Sabine C. Herpertz. "Understanding Brain Mechanisms of Reactive Aggression." *Current Psychiatry Reports* 22, no. 12 (November 2020): 81. https://doi.org/10.1007/s11920-020-01208-6.

Biography. "Ketanji Brown Jackson." March 7, 2022. https://www.biography.com/law-figure/ketanji-brown-jackson.

Blair, Robert James R. "Considering Anger from a Cognitive Neuroscience Perspective." *Wiley Interdisciplinary*

Reviews: Cognitive Science 3, no. 1 (January 2012): 65–74. https://doi.org/10.1002/wcs.154.

Brown, Brené. *Atlas of the Heart: Mapping Meaningful Connection and the Language of Human Experience.* New York: Random House, 2021.

California Scholarship Federation. "CSF Membership." Accessed July 13, 2022. https://csf-cjsf.org/membership/.

Caprino, Kathy. "What Selling 3 Million Copies of 'The Dance of Anger' Has Taught Renowned Psychologist Harriet Lerner." April 23, 2014. https://www.forbes.com/sites/kathycaprino/2014/04/23/what-selling-3-million-copies-of-the-dance-of-anger-has-taught-renowned-psychologist-harriet-lerner/.

Chodron, Pema. *When Things Fall Apart: Heart Advice for Difficult Times.* Boston: Shambhala Publications, Inc., 2000.

Damasio, Antonio, and Gil B. Carvalho. "The Nature of Feelings: Evolutionary and Neurobiological Origins." *Nature Reviews Neuroscience* 14 (January 2013): 143–152. https://doi.org/10.1038/nrn3403.

Denson, Thomas F. "The Multiple Systems Model of Angry Rumination." *Personality and Social Psychology Review* 17, no. 2 (November 2012): 103–23. https://doi.org/10.1177/1088868312467086.

Dr. Gabor Maté. "When the Body Says No: The Cost of Hidden Stress." Accessed June, 30, 2022. https://drgabormate.com/book/when-the-body-says-no/.

Feuerstein, Georg. *Tantra: The Path of Ecstasy.* Boston: Shambhala Publications, Inc., 1998.

Gilam, Gadi, and Talma Hendler. "Deconstructing Anger in the Human Brain." In *Social Behavior from Rodents to Humans,* edited by M. Wöhr and S. Krach, 257-73. Vol. 30 of *Current Topics in Behavioral Neurosciences.* New York: Springer, 2015.

Guiding Light Counseling (@guidinglight_counseling). Quote by Liza Palmer. *Instagram.* December 15, 2021. https://www.instagram.com/p/CXgd3jfLqwL/.

Hay, Louise L. *Heart Thoughts: A Treasury of Inner Wisdom.* Carlsbad, CA: Hay House, 2012.

Judiciary Committee. "Report on the Nomination of the Honorable Ketanji Brown Jackson to the Supreme Court of the United States." New York City Bar. April 1, 2022. https://www.nycbar.org/member-and-career-services/committees/reports-listing/reports/detail/nomination-of-judge-ketanji-brown-jackson.

Kim, Eun Joo, Blake Pellman, and Jeansok J. Kim. "Stress Effects on the Hippocampus: A Critical Review." *Learning & Memory* 22, no. 9 (2015): 411–416. https://doi.org/10.1101/lm.037291.114.

Lamott, Anne. "There are no words . . .," Facebook. May 25, 2022. https://z-p3-upload.facebook.com/AnneLamott/posts/556364802518697.

Litvak, Paul M., Jennifer S. Lerner, Larissa Z. Tiedens, and Katherine Shonk. "Fuel in the Fire: How Anger Impacts Judgment and Decision-Making." In *International Handbook of Anger*, edited by Michael Potegal, Gerhard Stemmler, and Charles Spielberger, 287-310. New York: Springer, 2010.

Menakem, Resmaa. *My Grandmother's Hands: Racialized Trauma and the Pathway to Mending Our Hearts and Bodies*. Las Vegas: Central Recovery Press, 2017.

Mookerjee, Ajit. *Kali: The Feminine Force*. Rochester, VT: Destiny Books, 1998.

Ramsland, Katherine. *The Vampire Companion: The Official Guide to Anne Rice's "The Vampire Chronicles."* New York: Ballantine Books, 1993.

Rice, Anne. *The Queen of the Damned*. New York: Ballantine Books, 1998.

Sophia, Anaiya. *Fierce Feminine Rising: Heal from Predatory Relationships and Recenter Your Personal Power*. Rochester, VT: Destiny Books, 2020.

Vanessa Alfaro. "Vanessa Alfaro." Accessed July 2, 2022. https://vanessaalfaro.co/.

Walker, Jay. "My Library of Human Imagination." Filmed
    2008. TED video, 6:50. https://www.ted.com/talks/
    jay_walker_my_library_of_human_imagination?lan-
    guage=en.

Wikipedia. "Who's Who Among American High School
    Students." Last modified January 22, 2022. https://
    en.wikipedia.org/wiki/Who%27s_Who_Among_
    American_High_School_Students.

Wikipedia. "Will Smith—Chris Rock slapping incident." Last
    modified January 29, 2022. https://en.wikipedia.org/
    wiki/Will_Smith%E2%80%93Chris_Rock_slapping_
    incident.

Winterich, Karen Page, Seunghee Han, and Jennifer S.
    Lerner. "Now that I'm Sad, It's Hard to be Mad: The
    Role of Cognitive Appraisals in Emotional Blunt-
    ing." *Personality & Social Psychology Bulletin* 36,
    no. 11 (September 2010): 1467–83, https://doi.
    org/10.1177/0146167210384710.

ABOUT THE CONTRIBUTORS

Abby Sommerfeld has a healthy respect for anger. As a life coach, writer, teacher, and mother, she sees it up close and personal every day. She studies its causes and consequences and understands its universal complexity. Her writing and coaching explore how to find our way in the world through both resonance and opposition. With humility and a sense of humor, Sommerfeld writes about anxiety; fear; hopes; dreams; and how to achieve a grounded connection to work, family, and oneself. This unique writing project offered an opportunity to look within herself and examine her own relationship to anger. She lives in San Francisco with her husband and son.

Audrey Katherine is a clinical psychologist and provides therapeutic services for marginalized populations. She's also involved in research for psychedelic-assisted therapy. Audrey uses the Internal Family Systems framework and the Anger Algorithm as tools for healing. She has a passion for electronic dance music and enjoys DJing and dancing. Audrey is walking on a mystical path. The opportunity to contribute to this book came at a perfect time to help integrate the inner work she's doing to release anger and heal trauma.

Cara Carrillo finds herself living in Tucson (land of Tohono, O'odham), Arizona, after growing up in New York and spending twenty-plus years in the Bay Area, California. A coach, consultant, and death doula, she's comfortable exploring what's just below the surface, except for when she's in avoidance and has to forgive herself. She's interested in community and how we can move toward a more sustainable, just, and equitable future together. You can find her roaming in the magical Sonoran Desert wash looking for bounty; cooking delicious vegan meals; cuddling with her dog; and communing with the spirits through tarot, visioning, and other mediums.

Carolina Lasso is the marketing director at SIY Global, author of the Amazon bestseller *The Path to Flourishing: Seven Principles for a Joyful, Fulfilling, and Purposeful Life*, and the creator of the Spanish language personal development platform Plenitud. Passionate about creating practical tools to help organizations and individuals flourish, Carolina combines her business background with her passion for personal development as a teacher, marketer, and consultant. She holds a bachelor's degree in international business from the University of Maryland and an MBA from New York University, and she has worked at Google, American Express, and Telemundo. Carolina is a certified Search Inside Yourself teacher, a mindfulness facilitator, and a marketing instructor. She enjoys oil painting, Latin dancing, spending time with her family in her native Colombia, and discovering new places around the world.

Chloe Rowshani is an Iranian American and California native born and raised in a beach town in Southern California and living nearly the last decade in San Francisco. Her never-ending thirst for learning has led to a mosaic of a career journey, a constant drive to explore and see new parts of the world, and a wide collection of hobbies that she is fine sucking at as long as she's still having fun.

Chrystal Bell loves good questions, the natural world, and uncovering hidden things. She's intensely interested in life's mysteries and human connection, which led her to careers in forensic science and executive coaching and facilitation. She came to this project because she could not resist a deep dive into the challenging territory of anger. Chrystal lives with her partner and their two children in the Pacific Northwest. She especially enjoys fine writing paper, good pens, and being in nature.

Dulcey Reiter spent her Southern California childhood swimming, reading, drawing, and looking for ladybugs in her parents' backyard. As a Jill-of-all-trades nonprofit communications professional with over twenty years of nonprofit experience, she's in the process of a career rethink focused on stopping the planet from overheating. Dulcey earned her master's degrees in international affairs and development and international studies from the George Washington University and the University of Sydney, respectively, spending several years abroad figuring out important things about the world. She enjoys costumed dance parties, freshly baked cookies, cocktails, and a good laugh. She currently lives with her husband, kids, and surly cat in the Bay Area.

Hideko Anderson was born and raised in a suburb outside the city of Seattle in the beautiful Pacific Northwest. She graduated from Western Washington University and majored in environmental studies and urban planning. Always fascinated with how cities work and how people interact with one another, she has recently taken an interest in her own emotions and programming. Understanding her ways of being, what runs her, and where it's rooted has been extremely important and led her to the topic of anger and her relationship to it. Now residing in the Bay Area, you can find her journaling, listening to music, or walking around Lake Merritt.

Kat Pedersen is a woman who has tried many things. Until recently, feeling her anger wasn't one of them, but this project has opened her eyes to its wisdom, thanks in large part to the amazing women who joined her on this journey. Before settling down with her fiancé in Austin, Texas, she lived in Switzerland, France, Ireland, and San Francisco. Once upon a time, she also earned a degree in finance and an MBA, only to learn that she wanted nothing to do with the business world. Now, she's pursuing a master's degree in counseling so she can earn her license in marriage and family therapy. Along the way, she's learning to love her anger.

Katie Karlson is a strong, creative teenager who loves art and video games. She loves spending time with her family, her parents' partners, her friends, and her wonderful cats. She loves food with most of her heart, but her favorite is pizza. She also loves baking and making wonderful things.

Lexi Lightwood is a fourteen-year-old who loves reading, writing, and hanging out with her friends. She is a second degree blackbelt in mixed martial arts. Her favorite animal is her pet cat, and she has a younger sister.

Lindsey Kugel is the executive director of the Search Inside Yourself leadership institute, where she gets to be part of a team that practices and offers mindfulness tools for those working in public service and activism. This work has, perhaps counterintuitively, helped her get more acquainted with her anger and other important emotions that need attention. She holds an MBA in sustainable business and is driven to create change for good. Her most potent practice is being a dedicated mom to her two inquisitive kids and a loving partner to her spouse, Uri. They live with their effusive dog, Jimi, in San Diego.

Lynn Bromley is a consultant, author, and speaker. She is fascinated by change and inspired by small acts of courage. At different times in her career, she has been a waitress, a teacher, a truck driver, a corporate manager, and a social worker. In 2000, she was elected to the Maine State Senate where she served four terms and was later appointed to the Obama Administration as New England's Small Business Advocate. She's the founder and principal at Fintech Advocate consulting and recently published her first book, *On the Path to Justice: The Dangerous Myth of Empowerment for Women*. As a traveler, agitator, and champion of innovators, she's a global citizen and frequent visitor to kjæresten hennes in Oslo, Norway, but lives mostly in South Portland, Maine, near her two children and a great gang of sisters. She has been a woman throughout all her iterations and is at the same time a fresh and learned voice on gender politics and justice.

Madeline McClure lives on colonized Tohono O'odham and Pascua Yaqui lands, otherwise known as Tucson, Arizona. She's a creative writing school dropout and shares most of her words anonymously in public spaces. Beyond writing, she enjoys being out in the desert with her dogs, taking windy drives to loud music, and learning from and fighting for social movements within and beyond the Americas.

Mary Anker initially resisted the idea of writing about anger and then couldn't stop thinking about it. Usually a writer of poetry, this challenging essay opportunity became an inner therapy trip and, surprisingly, a mini memoir. Several of Anker's poems have appeared in anthologies. Three poems, "I, Too, Sing the Piscataqua," "Cancer Creations," and "All the Poets Say What Love Is," won awards. Her first book, *an unlikely conversation*, is co-written with a former student, Will Grant. She loves open mikes and any chance to perform her poetry. She lives in New Hampshire with her husband, Art.

Mary Clare Wojcik is an ordained minister, personal development coach, mindfulness teacher, and peace advocate. She's author of the book, *Awakened Faith: Learning to Live the Lord's Prayer*. Mary Clare is also a Search Inside Yourself facilitator and Emotional Intelligence consultant. Through coaching, consultation, and retreats, Mary Clare helps individuals and organizations meet the world with their best selves, finding balance between the head, heart, and awakened awareness. She weaves the message of love, peace, compassion, and raising consciousness through every aspect of her work. Cultivate peace within and share it freely with the world around you. Mary Clare resides in Wisconsin and enjoys yoga, meditation, international travel, golf, and spending time with her family.

Mel Hilario is an alumna of Mills College, a daughter and granddaughter of immigrants, a recovering Catholic, a teller of stories, and a teacher of movement. She arrived at this project because she's been infuriated most of her life and didn't admit it until recently. To curtail her rage, she kicks and punches inanimate objects; indulges in good food and strong cocktails; and spends time with the smartest, most courageous, and trouble-makingest women she knows. Her two cats have helped her create her current mantra: feed me, love me, and leave me alone. She lives and writes in Oakland.

Mel Saavedra is a daughter, sister, mama, and collaborator based in Oakland. She finds joy and liberation through activism, social justice, creativity, art, fun/pleasure, practicing emergence, and healthy friction. She's traveled a winding path to becoming a life coach, facilitator, educator, yoga teacher/practitioner, and survivor. Her life's work and most powerful activism is as a parent, which is in direct resistance/recreation of intergenerational trauma on both sides of her heritage. Her father is Mexicano; her mother originates from Saigon, Vietnam. Her great grandfather Albino was a Yaqui healer, a curandero, a lineage she proudly calls in. She was excitedly intrigued by this project as a woman who embraces anger as disruptor, energizer, and catalyst for healing in all parts of her intersectional identity, alongside many emotions across a wide spectrum that has led to her becoming a fiercely honest, sometimes funny, and deeply loving leader.

Nicole Frances Williams was born and raised in the Bay Area. She's a social worker; former journalist; and nonprofit leader dedicated to helping women, children, and families in crisis. Nicole's search for healing and resilience has taken her across the country and around the world. In 2014, she completed the nearly 600-mile Camino de Santiago pilgrimage, which left her broken down and ready for the soul work that can only happen in therapy. As traumatic as Nicole's childhood was, she's proud and grateful to have a family willing to grow, change, and never stop fighting for each other. Nicole was drawn to this project on the heels of her divorce—a time of reckoning, a time to stop fighting alone and instead commune with her fellow Angry Women.

Rachael Sirianni, PhD, lives in Massachusetts with her husband (Greg), their three children (Jack, Wes, and Ada), and ever-growing menagerie of pets. She's also professor and vice chair of research in neurosurgery at the UMass Chan Medical School. Her research program focuses on the development of new therapies to treat diseases that affect the brain and spinal cord. Of all of the emotions, anger is the one she feels she understands the least.

Steph Stern is a coach and facilitator with a passion for supporting people to be their best in life and at work. She brings all of herself to her coaching work, including wisdom and struggles from a many-years long and ongoing personal growth journey, years of experience as a leader and nonprofit director in the wellness field, and an obsession with self-improvement schemes. She also loves fresh pens, leisurely mornings, and dark chocolate. Steph believes that there's no end to the amount of self-compassion that we all deserve, though applying it to her own anger has been more challenging. She lives in the Bay Area with a wonderful partner.

Tiffany Pham (she/they) is a second-generation Vietnamese American, queer empath residing on occupied Ohlone land. She's a life coach at Path and Present, where she enjoys working with tenderhearted humans and those who identify as QTBIPOC. Prior to becoming a coach, she worked in marketing and communications at startups for a decade. Tiffany was excited to join this project to explore the depths of her anger as a queer woman of color and to have a space where she could be unapologetically vulnerable in a community. She hopes to inspire others to do the same for themselves. In her free time, she enjoys meditation, hiking, and traveling with her partner, Laura.

Yolanda Marin-Czachor is a former teacher from New York City, where she received her master's degree from Teachers College, Columbia University. She has spent the last decade of her life raising her blended family in Wisconsin and is now looking forward to a calmer, quieter life among the rolling hills and magical mountains of North Carolina. A native of Central America, Yolanda loves to find new ways to blend the rituals of her ancestors with the grit of her former city life. Moving to the countryside is a dream come true because it gives her the opportunity to do both. In her free time, you can find her meditating among the trees and/or muttering to herself as she learns to garden.

www.ingramcontent.com/pod-product-compliance
Lightning Source LLC
Chambersburg PA
CBHW062052270326

41931CB00013B/3043